Better Homes and Gardens®

# His Turn to Cook


First Edition. Fourth Printing, 1984.
Library of Congress Catalog Card Number: 82-80527
ISBN: 0-696-00877-7 (hard cover)
ISBN: 0-696-00875-0 (trade paperback

**HIS TURN TO COOK**
Editors: Rosemary C. Hutchinson, Alethea Sparks
Copy and Production Editor: Lamont Olson
Graphic Designer: Mike Eagleton

**On the cover:**
*Steak and Bacon Tournedos* (see recipe, page 28)

BETTER HOMES AND GARDENS TEST KITCHEN™

Our seal assures you that every recipe in *His Turn to Cook* is endorsed by the Better Homes and Gardens Test Kitchen. Each recipe is tested for family appeal, practicality, and deliciousness.

# Contents

# Devil's Delight Chili

| | |
|---|---|
| **5 slices bacon** | ● In a large saucepan or Dutch oven cook bacon till crisp; drain and crumble. |
| **8 ounces Italian sausage links, sliced** | ● Brown sausage in the same saucepan. Drain sausage, reserving 2 tablespoons drippings; set sausage aside. |
| **2 medium onions**<br>**1 small green pepper**<br>**1½ pounds beef chuck steak, diced**<br>**1 clove garlic, minced** | ● Chop onions and green pepper. In reserved drippings cook chopped onion, chopped green pepper, diced beef, and minced garlic till meat is brown. |
| **2 dried red chili peppers, seeded and crumbled**<br>**2 jalapeño peppers, seeded and chopped**<br>**1 to 1½ tablespoons chili powder**<br>**½ teaspoon dried oregano, crushed**<br>**1 12-ounce can tomato paste** | ● Add crumbled bacon, cooked sliced sausage, dried red chili peppers, jalapeño peppers, chili powder, dried oregano, and ½ teaspoon *salt*. Stir in tomato paste and 2½ cups *water*.<br>Bring to boiling; reduce heat. Simmer, covered, 1½ hours, stirring occasionally. |
| **1 16-ounce can pinto beans, drained**<br>**1 16-ounce can garbanzo beans, drained** | ● Stir in pinto beans and garbanzo beans; simmer, covered, 30 minutes more. Makes 8 servings. |

**"It's not for the faint of heart or stomach," said the cook who sent us this recipe, and a glance at the ingredients will convince you. Italian sausage, dried red chili peppers, jalapeño peppers, and a whopping 1½ tablespoons of chili powder add to this chili's spicy punch. If you don't think your stomach is up to a chili this hot, start with 1 teaspoon chili powder. Then gradually increase it each time you make the recipe.**

Bell Pepper
Serrano Peppers
California or Green
Chili Peppers

# Meatball Chili

**2 hard-cooked eggs**

● Separate hard-cooked egg yolks from egg whites. Chop each separately.

**½ cup cooked brown rice**
**¼ cup soft bread crumbs**
**¼ cup sliced green onion**
**¼ cup chopped pitted ripe olives**
**¼ teaspoon dried rosemary, crushed**
**Dash ground cloves**
**Dash ground cinnamon**
**½ pound ground beef**
**½ pound ground pork**
**Raisins**

● In a bowl combine the chopped egg yolks, cooked brown rice, soft bread crumbs, the ¼ cup sliced green onion, the ¼ cup chopped ripe olives, rosemary, cloves, and cinnamon. Add ground beef and pork; mix well.

Using about 2 tablespoons of the meat mixture for each meatball, wrap the mixture around two or three raisins and shape into a 1½-inch ball.

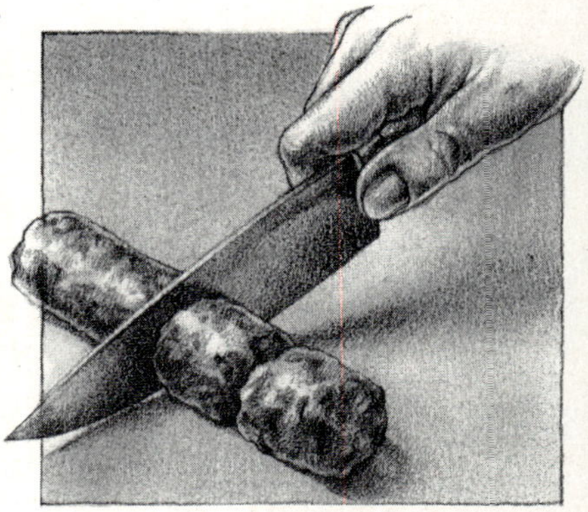

**Shaping meatballs is a snap if you keep this tip in mind. Form the meat mixture into a roll with a diameter the same as the diameter of the meatballs you need. Cut off 1½-inch slices and round them into balls or shape them around a filling.**

**2 cups water**
**1 10¾-ounce can condensed tomato soup**
**1 tablespoon chili powder**
**1 teaspoon instant beef bouillon granules**

● In a large saucepan combine the water, tomato soup, chili powder, instant beef bouillon granules, and meatballs. Bring to boiling. Reduce heat; simmer, covered, 30 minutes. Stir in chopped hard-cooked egg whites.

**½ cup shredded cheddar cheese (2 ounces)**
**Chopped pitted ripe olives**
**Sliced green onion**

● To serve, ladle chili into soup bowls; top each serving with some of the shredded cheddar cheese, additional olives, and green onion. Makes 4 to 6 servings.

# Vegetarian Chili

**2 medium zucchini**
**¼ cup sliced green onion**
**2 cloves garlic, minced**
**2 tablespoons cooking oil**

● Chop the zucchini. In a 5-quart Dutch oven cook the chopped zucchini, sliced green onion, and minced garlic in hot cooking oil till vegetables are tender.

**2 28-ounce cans tomatoes, cut up**
**3 15½-ounce cans red kidney beans**
**1 15-ounce can garbanzo beans**
**1 cup beer *or* water**
**½ cup peanuts**
**¼ cup vinegar**
**1 tablespoon chili powder**
**1½ teaspoons dried basil, crushed**
**1 teaspoon dried thyme, crushed**
**¼ teaspoon crushed red pepper**
**1 bay leaf**
**2 cups shredded Monterey Jack cheese (8 ounces)**

● Stir in the *undrained* tomatoes, *undrained* kidney beans, *undrained* garbanzo beans, beer or water, peanuts, vinegar, chili powder, dried basil, dried thyme, crushed red pepper, and bay leaf.

Bring to boiling; reduce heat. Cover and simmer chili for 30 minutes. Remove cover; simmer 1 hour longer.

Remove and discard bay leaf. Spoon chili into soup bowls. Top each serving of chili with ¼ cup of the shredded Monterey Jack cheese. Makes 8 servings.

**Meatless meals offer an interesting change of pace, and with careful planning they can be nutritionally well balanced. Combine grains with legumes, seeds, or nuts. Or serve dairy products with legumes, seeds, nuts, or grains.**

# Portuguese Kale Soup

| | |
|---|---|
| **2/3 cup dry red kidney beans**<br>**12 cups water** | ● Rinse beans. In a Dutch oven or kettle combine beans and *6 cups* of the water. Bring to boiling. Reduce heat; simmer 2 minutes. Remove from heat. Cover; let stand 1 hour. (Or, soak beans in water overnight in a covered pan.) Drain and rinse. In the same Dutch oven or kettle combine rinsed beans and the remaining 6 cups water. |
| **1 pound beef shank crosscuts**<br>**8 ounces linguisa, chorizo, or bulk Italian sausage**<br>**2/3 cup dry split peas**<br>**2½ teaspoons salt** | ● In a skillet brown beef shank crosscuts and sausage; drain well. Stir into *undrained* beans along with dry split peas and salt. Bring to boiling; reduce heat. Simmer, covered, 2 hours.<br>Remove beef shanks. When cool enough to handle, remove meat from bones; cube. Discard bones; return meat to Dutch oven. |
| **6 cups torn kale**<br>**2 medium potatoes, peeled and chopped**<br>**2 cups chopped cabbage** | ● Add torn kale, chopped potatoes, and chopped cabbage. Simmer, covered, 25 to 30 minutes more. Spoon into soup bowls. Makes 8 to 10 servings. |

## Freeze It

To save time, freeze chilies, soups, or stews in 1-,2-, or 4-cup portions. Then when you need a quick supper, thaw one in your microwave oven. Place the frozen mixture in a bowl or a 1- or 1½-quart casserole. Micro-cook, on HIGH, covered, for 2 minutes (for 1-cup portion); 3 minutes (for 2-cup portion); or 4 minutes (for 4-cup portion). Break up the semi-frozen mixture. Cook, covered for 4, 7, or 12 minutes more, depending on the portion size. Stir several times during the final cooking.

**Portuguese Kale Soup is standard fare for many Portuguese-American families. What makes it unusual is the use of fresh kale and a Portuguese sausage, linguisa. If you can't find these ingredients in your area, use spinach in place of the kale and bulk Italian sausage in place of the linguisa.**

# Oyster-Wine Chowder

| | |
|---|---|
| **2 medium onions, chopped (1 cup)**<br>**2 tablespoons snipped parsley**<br>**2 tablespoons butter** | ● In a large saucepan cook the chopped onion and the snipped parsley in butter till onion is tender but not brown. |
| **1 tablespoon soy sauce**<br>**1 teaspoon dried thyme, crushed**<br>**1 bay leaf**<br>**Dash bottled hot pepper sauce**<br>**1 pint shucked oysters** | ● Stir in the soy sauce, dried thyme, bay leaf, and bottled hot pepper sauce. Add the oysters; cook and stir over low heat about 5 minutes or till the edges of the oysters begin to curl. |
| **2 cups milk**<br>**½ cup light cream**<br>**2 cups shredded American cheese (8 ounces)** | ● Stir in milk and light cream. Heat through. Add shredded American cheese, stirring till cheese is melted. |
| **⅓ cup dry white wine** | ● Remove from heat; discard bay leaf. Stir in white wine. Makes 6 servings. |

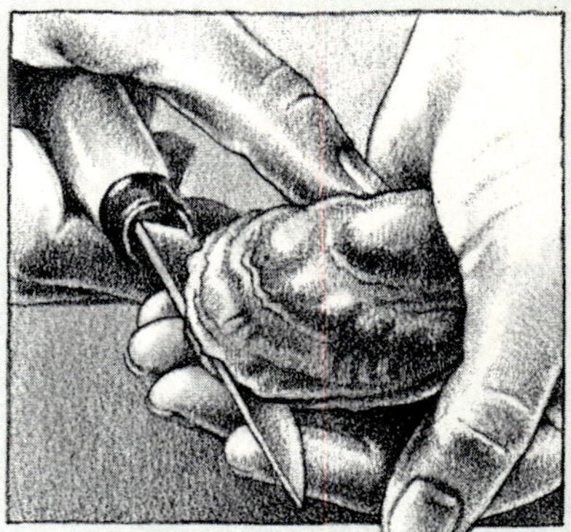

**If you gather your own oysters or want to try oysters on the half-shell, here's how to shuck them. Hold each shell firmly and insert an oyster knife between the halves, twisting slightly upward.**

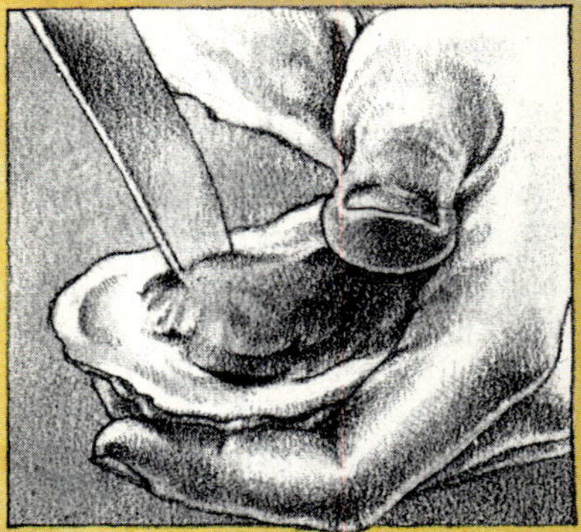

**Once the shell is partially open, cut around the opening and pry the shell completely open. Pull the top half up and cut the oyster free.**

**The key to a good oyster stew is preparing the oysters properly. Cook them only until the edges begin to curl, usually about 5 minutes.**

# Lamb Cassoulet

**2 cups dry navy beans**
**8 cups water**

● Rinse beans. In Dutch oven mix the 8 cups water and beans. Bring to boiling. Reduce heat; simmer 2 minutes. Remove from heat. Do not drain. Cover; let stand 1 hour. (Or, add water to beans. Cover; let stand overnight.)

**6 cups water**
**1 pound boneless lamb, cut into 1-inch cubes**
**1 cup chopped carrot**
**½ cup chopped green pepper**
**½ cup chopped onion**
**1 tablespoon instant beef bouillon granules**
**¼ teaspoon garlic powder**
**¾ pound bulk pork sausage**

● Drain beans; rinse. In Dutch oven mix rinsed beans and the 6 cups water. Add lamb, vegetables, bouillon granules, and garlic powder. Bring to boiling; reduce heat. Simmer, covered, for 1½ hours.

Meanwhile, shape pork sausage into small balls; brown in a large skillet.

Drain bean mixture, reserving liquid. Return bean mixture to Dutch oven. Skim fat from reserved bean liquid.

**1 16-ounce can tomatoes, cut up**
**1 tablespoon Worcestershire sauce**
**2 bay leaves**
**1 teaspoon dried savory, crushed**

● Add sausage balls, *undrained* tomatoes, Worcestershire sauce, bay leaves, savory, and ½ teaspoon *salt* to Dutch oven. Stir in *1 cup* of the bean liquid. Cover; bake in a 325° oven for 1 to 1¼ hours. (Add more bean liquid if necessary.) Discard bay leaves. Skim fat. Makes 8 servings.

**Cassoulet is a French word meaning bean stew. Although many Frenchmen claim their version is the only authentic one, the term is used loosely to cover just about any concoction of white beans, lamb, and sausage.**

# South American Beef Soup

**2 pounds beef flank steak**
**1 tablespoon cooking oil**
**6 cups water**
**2 teaspoons salt**

● Cut beef flank steak into 1-inch slices. In a Dutch oven brown meat, half at a time, in cooking oil; drain.

Return all meat to pan; add the water and salt. Bring mixture to boiling; reduce heat. Simmer, covered, about 1¼ hours.

**2 medium carrots**
**2 onions**
**4 potatoes**
**1 10-ounce package frozen cut green beans**
**¼ cup chopped celery leaves**
**¼ cup snipped parsley**
**2 cloves garlic, minced**
**⅛ teaspoon crushed red pepper**
**8 ounces winter squash**
**¼ cup long grain rice**

● Cut carrots into 1-inch chunks. Cut onions into quarters. Peel and quarter potatoes. Add carrots, onions, potatoes, beans, chopped celery leaves, snipped parsley, garlic, crushed red pepper, and ¼ teaspoon *pepper* to meat mixture. Cover; simmer 10 minutes.

Cut squash into 8 pieces; add squash and rice to soup. Simmer 10 to 15 minutes or till vegetables and rice are tender.

Transfer meat and vegetables to platter. Spoon broth into 8 soup bowls; add ingredients from platter. Serves 8.

**Make this hearty soup your first of the fall season. Because it includes so many vegetables, it's a great way to use the harvest from your garden or the local farmer's market. Serve it in deep bowls with crusty French bread.**

# German-Style Pork Chowder

| | |
|---|---|
| **1 pound ground pork**<br>**½ cup chopped onion**<br>**½ cup chopped celery** | ● In medium saucepan cook ground pork, chopped onion, and chopped celery till meat is brown and vegetables are tender. Drain off fat. |
| **3 tablespoons all-purpose flour**<br>**¾ teaspoon salt**<br>**½ teaspoon caraway seed**<br>**3 cups milk** | ● Stir in all-purpose flour, salt, caraway seed, and ⅛ teaspoon *pepper*. Add milk all at once. Cook and stir till mixture is thickened and bubbly. Cook and stir 1 minute more. Reduce heat to simmer. |
| **1 8-ounce can sauerkraut**<br>**¾ cup shredded Swiss cheese (3 ounces)**<br>**2 tablespoons snipped parsley** | ● Rinse, drain, and snip sauerkraut. Stir sauerkraut, cheese, and parsley into meat mixture in saucepan; heat through, stirring till cheese is melted. Serves 5. |

**When you're looking for a different party idea—think soup. Make it ahead and chill it till party time. Then when guests arrive and it's time to eat, heat up the soup, set out the bowls, and let the guests help themselves. Finish off the meal with bread, and a quick dessert.**

# Chicken-Lentil Soup

| | |
|---|---|
| **1 2½- to 3-pound broiler fryer chicken, cut up**<br>**1 medium smoked pork hock (ham hock)**<br>**½ cup chopped onion**<br>**½ cup sliced celery**<br>**1½ teaspoons salt**<br>**¼ teaspoon pepper**<br>**8 cups water** | ● In a large saucepan or kettle combine chicken, pork hock, onion, celery, salt, and pepper. Add water; bring to boiling. Reduce heat. Cover; simmer 40 minutes.<br>Remove chicken and pork hock from kettle. When meats are cool enough to handle, remove meat from bones and coarsely chop. Discard bones. |
| **1½ cups dry lentils** | ● Return meat to kettle. Rinse lentils; add to kettle. Cover; simmer 20 minutes. |
| **2 medium carrots, sliced**<br>**2 medium potatoes, peeled and cubed**<br>**1½ cups shredded cabbage**<br>**1 10-ounce package frozen peas**<br>**1 cup dry white wine**<br>**½ teaspoon dried basil, crushed** | ● Stir in sliced carrots, cubed potatoes, shredded cabbage, peas, dry white wine, and dried basil.<br>Cover and simmer 10 minutes or till vegetables are tender. Season to taste with salt and pepper. Serves 8 to 10. |

**Pork hocks are a cut of meat taken from the lower legs of hogs. Since hocks are mostly bone and cartilage with little meat, they're an inexpensive way to add rich meat flavor to soups. You can buy them at most large supermarkets in fresh, pickled, cured, or smoked form. Smoked hocks may also be called ham hocks.**

# Pork-Vegetable Skillet

**1 pound boneless pork**
**2 tablespoons cooking oil**

● For easier cutting, partially freeze pork; cut into bite-size strips. In skillet brown pork in cooking oil; drain.

**2 cups beef broth**
**½ cup chopped onion**
**1 6-ounce package regular long grain and wild rice mix**
**1 cup sliced celery**
**1 cup sliced carrot**

● Add beef broth, chopped onion, and seasoning packet from rice mix. Stir in rice. Cover and simmer 10 minutes. Add celery and carrot and simmer 15 minutes longer or till meat and rice are tender. Makes 4 servings.

**To chop an onion, start by cutting it in half. Using the cut side as a stable base, slice each onion half in one direction. Then, hold the slices together and slice in the other direction.**

# Biscuit-Topped Stroganoff

**1 package (10) refrigerated biscuits**
**1 3-ounce package cream cheese with chives**

● Flatten biscuits with your hand. Divide cheese into 10 portions. Place one portion in center of each biscuit. Fold in half. Press edges to seal. Cover; set aside.

**1 pound ground beef**
**1½ cups sliced fresh mushrooms**
**½ cup chopped celery**
**½ cup chopped onion**
**1 clove garlic, minced**

● In skillet cook ground beef, sliced mushrooms, chopped celery, chopped onion, and minced garlic till beef is brown and onion is tender; drain.

**3 tablespoons all-purpose flour**
**1 cup milk**
**½ cup dairy sour cream**
**2 tablespoons dry sherry**
**½ teaspoon salt**
**⅛ teaspoon pepper**

● Stir flour into meat mixture. Add milk, sour cream, sherry, salt, and pepper. Cook and stir till mixture thickens and bubbles. Turn into a 1½-quart casserole.

Immediately top with biscuits. Bake in 450° oven 8 to 10 minutes or till biscuits are golden. Makes 4 or 5 servings.

**Confused by the many kinds of ground beef in the meat case? Just remember to buy the type that suits your recipe. Use 70 to 75 percent lean when you'll be draining the meat. When you want meat to be juicy, opt for 75 to 80 percent lean. For lower calorie meals, switch to 80 to 85 percent lean meat.**

# Tacos in a Dish

This casserole offers all the flavor of traditional tacos, without the hassle. Instead of worrying about assembling individual servings, layer all the ingredients in one dish.

| | |
|---|---|
| **1 16-ounce can stewed tomatoes**<br>**1 teaspoon sugar**<br>**¾ teaspoon dried oregano, crushed**<br>**½ teaspoon Worcestershire sauce**<br>**Several dashes bottled hot pepper sauce**<br>**¼ cup chopped green pepper**<br>**¼ cup chopped onion** | ● In a mixing bowl stir together the *undrained* stewed tomatoes, sugar, dried oregano, Worcestershire sauce, bottled hot pepper sauce, ¼ teaspoon *salt*, and ⅛ teaspoon *pepper*.<br>Using the edge of a spoon, break up large tomato pieces. Stir in the chopped green pepper and the chopped onion; set tomato mixture aside. |
| **1 pound chorizo *or* bulk Italian sausage** | ● In a medium skillet cook sausage till brown, stirring to break up large pieces of meat. Drain off fat. |
| **6 cups corn chips**<br>**4 *or* 5 slices American cheese** | ● Coarsely crush corn chips; place in the bottom of an ungreased 8x8x2-inch baking dish or 8x1½-inch round baking dish. Spoon hot meat over corn chips; top with cheese slices. |
| **2 cups shredded lettuce**<br>**Taco sauce (optional)** | ● Bake in a 350° oven for 10 to 12 minutes or till heated through and cheese begins to melt. Sprinkle casserole with shredded lettuce; spoon on tomato mixture. Serve immediately. Pass taco sauce if desired. Makes 4 to 6 servings. |

**MICROWAVE TIMING**
Micro-cook on HIGH, covered, for 3 to 4 minutes or till heated through.

# Savory Flank Steak

- **1 1- to 1½-pound beef flank steak *or* top round steak**
- **2 tablespoons catsup**
- **1 teaspoon sugar**
- **1 teaspoon Worcestershire sauce**
- **½ teaspoon dry mustard**
- **½ teaspoon minced dried onion**
- **¼ teaspoon celery seed**
- **⅛ teaspoon minced dried garlic**

● Score beef flank steak or top round steak on both sides.

In a small mixing bowl, combine the catsup, sugar, Worcestershire sauce, dry mustard, minced dried onion, celery seed, minced dried garlic, 2 tablespoons *water*, ½ teaspoon *salt,* and ⅛ teaspoon *pepper*. Set aside.

**Snipped parsley**

● Place meat on rack of unheated broiler pan; broil 3 to 4 inches from heat for 4 to 5 minutes. Brush meat with some of the catsup mixture; turn. Broil 4 to 5 minutes more for medium-rare doneness. Brush with remaining catsup mixture. Sprinkle with snipped parsley.

● To serve, thinly slice meat across the grain. Makes 4 to 6 servings.

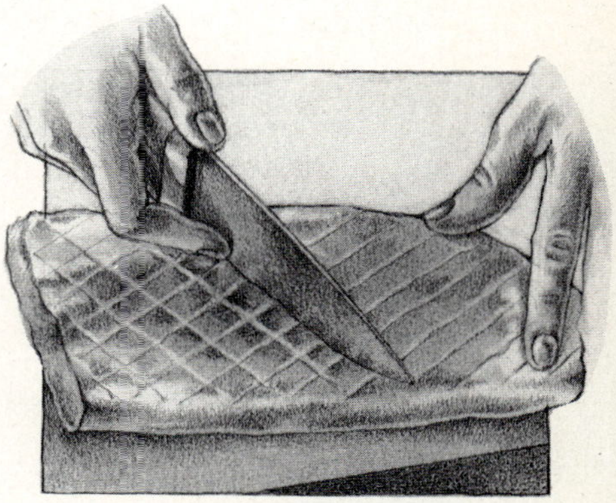

**To prevent the beef flank or top round steak from curling during broiling, make several shallow cuts in a crisscross fashion on each side of the steak.**

**Place the meat on the rack of an unheated broiler pan. (Using a cold pan keeps the steak from sticking to the surface.) Broil 3 to 4 inches from the heat.**

## Organization Tips

Get organized—that's the cardinal rule for serving meals on the double. First, plan meals for several days at a time. Then make a master grocery list. Second, arrange your kitchen so you can find things quickly. Having duplicate sets of utensils cuts down on mid-recipe dishwashing. Third, read recipes all the way through before you start so you will be familiar with all the ingredients and cooking procedures. Assemble everything you need before you begin. Finally, coordinate recipe steps to save time. For example, prepare a salad to go with Savory Flank Steak while the meat is broiling.

# Curry Powder

- ¼ cup ground coriander
- 3 tablespoons ground turmeric
- 2 tablespoons *each* ground cardamom, cumin, and fenugreek
- 2 teaspoons *each* pepper and ground red pepper
- 1 teaspoon *each* ground cinnamon, cloves, fennel, and ginger

If you like spicy food, curry-flavored dishes are probably high on your list of favorites. Curry powder is actually a blend of spices. Sometimes 16 or more different flavorings go into the blend, and many Far Eastern cooks make their own rather than relying on commercial products. If you'd like to try your hand at making curry powder, start by combining all the ingredients at left. Then improvise to suit your taste. This recipe makes ¾ cup curry powder.

# Curry Chicken Skillet

| | |
|---|---|
| **2 chicken breasts (1 pound)** | ● Skin and bone chicken breasts; cut into 1½-inch pieces. |
| **½ teaspoon curry powder**<br>**2 tablespoons butter *or* margarine** | ● In a medium skillet cook chicken and curry powder in butter or margarine till chicken is golden brown. |
| **1 10¾-ounce can condensed golden mushroom soup**<br>**1 tablespoon soy sauce**<br>**1 teaspoon Worcestershire sauce**<br>**½ teaspoon poppy seed** | ● Stir in the golden mushroom soup, soy sauce, Worcestershire sauce, poppy seed, and ½ cup *water*; mix well. Cover the skillet and simmer 10 minutes, stirring occasionally. |
| **1 8-ounce can bamboo shoots**<br>**1 3-ounce can sliced mushrooms**<br>**½ cup sliced celery** | ● Drain bamboo shoots and mushrooms. Add to soup mixture along with sliced celery. Cover skillet and simmer 5 minutes or till celery is crisp tender. |
| **1 6-ounce package frozen pea pods**<br>**3 tablespoons dry white wine**<br>**Hot cooked rice** | ● Stir in the pea pods and dry white wine; simmer, uncovered, 2 to 3 minutes more or till heated through. Serve over rice. Makes 4 to 6 servings. |

**Curry powder gives this 40-minute skillet supper a mildly spicy flavor and a distinctive yellow-gold color. Serve Curry Chicken Skillet over rice, the traditional accompaniment for curry dishes.**

# Skillet Sausage-Potato Salad

| | | |
|---|---|---|
| **4 Polish sausages *or* frankfurters, sliced** | ● In a large skillet cook sliced sausages or frankfurters over medium heat till brown; drain off fat if necessary. | **Served straight from the skillet, this main-dish potato salad can be on the table in 25 minutes. Or, if you like, turn it into a side dish by serving small portions in individual lettuce cups.** |
| **1 16-ounce can German-style potato salad**<br>**1 teaspoon prepared mustard** | ● Stir in the German-style potato salad and prepared mustard. Heat through. | |
| **1 cup shredded mozzarella, cheddar, muenster, *or* brick cheese (4 ounces)** | ● Remove the skillet from heat. Top sausage-potato salad mixture with shredded mozzarella, cheddar, muenster, or brick cheese. Makes 4 servings. | |

# Orange-Glazed Ham Slice

| | | |
|---|---|---|
| **1 1-pound ham slice, cut ½ to ¾ inch thick** | ● In a skillet cook the ham slice 8 to 10 minutes over medium-high heat, turning once till lightly brown. | |
| **½ cup orange marmalade**<br>**¼ cup dry white wine**<br>**1 tablespoon horseradish mustard** | ● Meanwhile, stir together the orange marmalade, dry white wine, and horseradish mustard; set aside. | **When meat and potatoes are the order of the day, this tasty ham dish goes together in just 20 minutes. To dress it up for company, trim the ham with a few thin slices of an orange.** |
| **1 17-ounce can sweet potatoes, drained** | ● Add drained sweet potatoes to skillet. Spoon the orange marmalade mixture over all. Cook, uncovered, 10 minutes over low heat or till ham and potatoes are glazed, spooning marmalade mixture over frequently. Makes 4 servings. | |

# Peloponnesian Pot Roast

| | |
|---|---|
| **1 2½- to 3-pound beef chuck pot roast**<br>**4 large cloves garlic, halved**<br>**¼ teaspoon salt** | ● Cut meat as necessary to fit into a 4-quart electric slow crockery cooker. Make 8 slits in roast; insert garlic. Sprinkle roast with salt and ⅛ teaspoon *pepper.* |
| **1 8-ounce can (1 cup) tomato sauce**<br>**1 tablespoon vinegar**<br>**¼ teaspoon ground nutmeg**<br>**¼ teaspoon ground cinnamon**<br>**⅛ teaspoon ground cloves** | ● In a bowl combine the tomato sauce, vinegar, ground nutmeg, cinnamon, and cloves. Pour tomato mixture over meat in crockery cooker.<br>Cover; cook on low heat setting for 8 to 10 hours. (*Or,* if desired, cook on high heat setting for 4 to 5 hours.) |
| **3 tablespoons cold water**<br>**2 tablespoons cornstarch** | ● Transfer meat to a serving platter; remove garlic halves. Keep meat warm.<br>Skim fat from juices in crockery cooker. Add water to juices, if necessary, to make 2 cups liquid. In a saucepan combine the 3 tablespoons water and cornstarch. Add the 2 cups liquid. Cook and stir till mixture is thickened and bubbly; cook 2 minutes more. |
| **Hot cooked spaghetti** | ● Slice meat; arrange atop spaghetti. Spoon some of the sauce over meat. Pass remaining sauce. Serves 6 to 8. |

**The four cloves of garlic in Peloponnesian Pot Roast give it a zesty flavor. To make sure the flavor penetrates the meat, make eight small evenly spaced cuts in the roast with the tip of a sharp knife. Then poke a garlic clove half in each.**

**Are you in for a long day? Here's a way to shorten it by trimming your meat preparation time. Use an automatic timer to start your crockery cooker while you're away from home. Before leaving, place the chilled food in your cooker. Cover it, then plug the cooker into an automatic timer and set the timer. Just be sure the food does not stand at room temperature for more than two hours before your crockery cooker comes on.**

## Crockery Cooker Care

Your electric slow crockery cooker is more delicate than it looks. Sudden temperature changes can crack or damage the ceramic liner. Don't put cold food in a hot cooker, and never put your cooker in the refrigerator or immerse it in water. The easiest way to clean the inside is with a soft cloth dipped in warm soapy water. (Do not use abrasive cleaners and cleansing pads.) If you add water to your cooker after the food is served, the remaining food won't harden on the sides and cleanup will be easier.

# Corned Beef Dinner

| | |
|---|---|
| **2 medium onions**<br>**3 medium potatoes**<br>**3 medium carrots**<br>**2 cloves garlic, minced**<br>**2 bay leaves** | ● Slice onions. Peel and quarter potatoes. Cut carrots into ½-inch chunks. In a 3½- to 4-quart electric slow crockery cooker layer onions, potatoes, carrots, garlic, and bay leaves. |
| **1 3-pound corned beef brisket**<br>**½ small head cabbage**<br>**½ cup water** | ● Trim fat from corned beef brisket. Place brisket atop vegetables. (Add herb packet, if present, along with liquid from the meat package.) Cut cabbage into 4 wedges. Place cabbage atop beef. Add water. Cover; cook on low heat setting for 7 to 8 hours. |
| **¼ cup packed brown sugar**<br>**1 tablespoon prepared mustard**<br>**Dash ground cloves** | ● In a bowl combine sugar, mustard, and cloves. Lift corned beef and place atop cabbage; spread with sugar mixture. Cover; cook 1 hour more. |
| **Parsley sprigs (optional)** | ● Slice meat and arrange on platter with vegetables. Garnish with parsley if desired. Makes 6 to 8 servings. |

**If a crockery cooker recipe cooks in 8 hours on the low heat setting, switch it to high heat and it will cook in 4 hours. Conversely, a recipe that cooks in 4 hours on high can cook in 8 on low.**

**To get all the ingredients cooked at the same time, put slow-cooking vegetables on the bottom so they are exposed to more heat.**

**Put the corned beef brisket atop the vegetables, so the meat won't stick to the bottom of the cooker.**

**Place the cabbage wedges on top because they need less heat to cook. Near the end of cooking put the meat on top to help steam the cabbage.**

# Basic Meat Loaf Mixture

| | |
|---|---|
| **2 beaten eggs**<br>**1½ cups soft bread crumbs**<br>**¼ cup milk**<br>**1½ teaspoons onion salt**<br>**1 teaspoon dried basil, thyme, *or* marjoram, crushed** | ● In a large bowl combine the beaten eggs; soft bread crumbs; milk; onion salt; choice of dried basil, thyme, or marjoram; and ¼ teaspoon *pepper.* |
| **1½ pounds lean ground beef** | ● Add ground beef; mix thoroughly. Use meat loaf mixture in any of the recipes on these two pages. |

# Mexi Meatballs

| | |
|---|---|
| **Basic Meat Loaf Mixture** | ● Prepare Basic Meat Loaf Mixture. Divide mixture into 12 portions. |
| **3 ounces pepper *or* cheddar cheese, cut into 12 (½-inch) cubes** | ● Wrap one portion of meat around each cheese cube, making a ball. Place one meatball in each of twelve 2½-inch muffin cups. Bake in a 350° oven for 20 minutes. Spoon off fat. |
| **⅓ cup bottled taco sauce** | ● Spoon taco sauce over each meatball. Bake 5 minutes more. Makes 6 servings. |

**For picture-perfect Barbecue Apple-Beef Pie (see recipe, right) build a high crust. That way when the meat shrinks during baking, the shell will still hold the apple filling. Pat the meat mixture high up the sides of the plate and patch any holes or cracks that appear as you work.**

# Barbecue-Style Apple-Beef Pie

**Basic Meat Loaf Mixture**

● Prepare Basic Meat Loaf Mixture. Press meat mixture over bottom and up the sides of a 9-inch pie plate to form a shell. (See tip, left.) Bake, uncovered, in a 350° oven for 30 minutes. Drain fat.

**½ cup chopped onion**
**2 tablespoons butter *or* margarine**
**1 cup catsup**
**½ cup packed brown sugar**
**2 tablespoons vinegar**
**2 teaspoons prepared mustard**
**1 20-ounce can sliced apples, drained**

● Meanwhile, in a saucepan cook the chopped onion in the butter or margarine till tender but not brown. Stir in the catsup, brown sugar, vinegar, and prepared mustard. Fold in drained apples. Heat through. Spoon apple mixture into prebaked meat shell. Bake, uncovered, 10 minutes more.

To serve, cut pie into wedges. Makes 6 servings.

**Shaping meat loaf into a ring makes it special enough for guests and reduces cooking time. Spoon the meat mixture into an ungreased 5½-cup ring mold. (Check the size of your mold by filling it with 5½ cups water.) Firmly pack the meat into the mold with your hand so it will hold the ring shape. Then unmold it into a 10-inch pie plate.**

# Lemon-Glazed Meat Ring

**Basic Meat Loaf Mixture**

● Prepare Basic Meat Loaf Mixture. Pat meat mixture into a 5½-cup ring mold. Unmold into a 10-inch pie plate.

Bake in a 350° oven for 50 minutes. Remove from oven; spoon off fat.

**½ cup packed brown sugar**
**2 tablespoons lemon juice**
**½ teaspoon dry mustard**

● In a bowl combine brown sugar, lemon juice, and mustard; spoon or brush over ring. Return meat ring to the oven for 10 minutes. Makes 6 servings.

| MEAT | + BROTH | + SEASONING | + DAIRY PRODUCT |
|---|---|---|---|
| **1½ pounds ground beef** | **1 tablespoon instant beef *or* chicken bouillon granules and 1⅓ cups water** | **½ teaspoon dried thyme, crushed** | **1 8-ounce carton dairy sour cream *or* one 8-ounce can imitation sour cream** |
| **1½ pounds ground pork** | **1 10¾-ounce can condensed chicken broth** | **½ teaspoon dried oregano, crushed** | **1 8-ounce carton plain yogurt** |
| **1½ pounds ground lamb** | **1 10½-ounce can condensed beef broth** | **½ teaspoon dried basil, crushed** | **1 8-ounce carton sour cream dip with chives** |
| **1½ pounds ground veal** | | **½ teaspoon dried marjoram, crushed** | **1 8-ounce package cream cheese, softened** |
| **1½ pounds ground turkey** | | **½ teaspoon dried savory, crushed** | |

On those nights when you forget to plan something for dinner, don't head for the nearest fast-food place. Look in your kitchen. You probably have the makings for at least one of the delicious recipes on the next four pages. They're designed so you can mix and match ingredients. Pick one option from each column. Add them to the list of base ingredients, and you're ready to cook a delicious main dish.

# Mix 'n' Match Meatballs

**+ STARCH**

**Hot cooked noodles**

**Hot cooked spaghetti**

**Hot cooked elbow macaroni**

**Hot cooked rice**

**Hot cooked spaetzle**

**+ ALL OF THESE =**

- **2 beaten eggs**
- **¼ cup milk**
- **1½ cups soft bread crumbs (about 2½ slices)**
- **¼ teaspoon salt**
- **½ cup chopped onion**
- **1 tablespoon cooking oil**
- **1 4-ounce can mushroom stems and pieces**
- **2 tablespoons all-purpose flour**
- **Snipped parsley**

● In a bowl combine the eggs and milk. Stir in bread crumbs and salt.

● Add your choice of ground meat; mix well. Shape into about 60 (1-inch) meatballs. Place in shallow baking pan. Bake in a 375° oven for 25 to 30 minutes or till done. Drain on paper toweling.

● In a large skillet cook onion in hot oil till tender but not brown.

● Add meatballs to skillet along with your choice of broth and seasoning. Cover; simmer 10 minutes.

● Remove meatballs from pan juices; skim fat. Add undrained mushrooms. Bring to boiling; reduce heat.

● Stir flour into sour cream, yogurt, dip, or cream cheese. (If using cream cheese, stir in 2 tablespoons water with the flour. If using yogurt, use 3 tablespoons flour.)

● Add flour mixture to pan juices. Cook and stir till thickened and bubbly. Add meatballs; heat through. Serve over hot noodles, spaghetti, macaroni, rice, or spaetzle. Top with parsley. Serves 6.

| SAUCE | + ONION | + MEAT | + PASTA |
|---|---|---|---|
| 1 8-ounce can pizza sauce | ½ cup chopped onion | 2 cups cubed cooked beef | 2 cups cooked elbow macaroni |
| 1 8-ounce can tomato sauce | 1 tablespoon minced dried onion | 2 cups cubed cooked pork | 2 cups cooked fine noodles |
| 1 cup bottled spaghetti sauce | ½ teaspoon onion powder | 2 cups cubed fully cooked ham | 2 cups cooked tiny shell macaroni |
| | | 2 cups cubed cooked chicken | 2 cups cooked rigatoni |
| | | 2 cups cubed cooked turkey | 2 cups cooked cavatelli |

| MEAT | + BROTH | + LIQUID SEASONING | + DRY SEASONING |
|---|---|---|---|
| 1½ pounds beef stew meat, cut into 1-inch cubes | 1 13¾-ounce can beef broth | 1 tablespoon Worcestershire sauce | 1 teaspoon dried thyme, crushed |
| 1½ pounds pork stew meat, cut into 1-inch cubes | 1 teaspoon instant beef bouillon granules *and* 1½ cups water | 1 tablespoon soy sauce | 1 teaspoon dried basil, crushed |
| 1½ pounds lamb stew meat, cut into 1-inch cubes | 1 13¾-ounce can chicken broth | 1 teaspoon prepared horseradish | 1 teaspoon dried marjoram, crushed |
| 1 2½- to 3-pound broiler-fryer chicken, cut up | 2 teaspoons instant chicken bouillon granules *and* 1½ cups water | 1 teaspoon prepared mustard | 1 teaspoon dried oregano, crushed |

# Create-a-Casserole

**+ CHEESE**

- **½ cup shredded mozzarella cheese**
- **½ cup shredded cheddar cheese**
- **½ cup shredded Monterey Jack cheese**
- **½ cup shredded brick cheese**
- **½ cup shredded American cheese**

**+ ALL OF THESE =**

**1 tablespoon butter *or* margarine**
**2 tablespoons all-purpose flour**
**1 16-ounce can stewed tomatoes *or* tomatoes, cut up**
**¼ cup water**
**Dash pepper**

● In a large saucepan melt butter or margarine. Stir in flour.
● Stir in undrained tomatoes, your choice of sauce, onion or onion powder, water, and pepper. (If using tomato or pizza sauce, add ½ teaspoon dried oregano, crushed.)
● Cook and stir till mixture is thickened and bubbly.
● Stir in your choice of meat and pasta.
● Turn into a 2-quart casserole.
● Bake, uncovered, in a 350° oven for 20 minutes.
● Sprinkle your choice of cheese atop. Bake 5 minutes more or till cheese melts. Serves 4 or 5.

# Stir-Up-a-Stew

**+ VEGETABLES**

**5 cups chopped, sliced, *or* cubed vegetables (carrots, celery, green pepper, onions, parsnips, potatoes, rutabagas, *or* turnips)**

**+ ALL OF THESE =**

**¼ cup all-purpose flour**
**½ teaspoon salt**
**¼ teaspoon pepper**
**2 tablespoons cooking oil**
**1 bay leaf**
**¾ teaspoon salt**
**¼ cup water**
**2 tablespoons all-purpose flour**

● In a plastic bag combine the ¼ cup flour, ½ teaspoon salt, and pepper.
● Add half of desired meat at a time to bag, shaking to coat well. (Shake a few pieces of chicken at a time.)
● In Dutch oven cook meat, half at a time, in hot oil till lightly brown. Drain off fat. Return all meat to pan.
● Add your choice of broth, liquid seasoning, dry seasoning, the bay leaf, and the ¾ teaspoon salt to Dutch oven.
● Bring mixture to boiling; reduce heat. Simmer, covered, 1 hour for beef, pork, and lamb; 30 minutes for chicken or till meat is tender.
● Add 5 cups assorted vegetables. Cover and simmer 30 minutes more or till the vegetables are tender.
● (If using chicken, transfer pieces to platter; keep warm.) Combine the ¼ cup water and the 2 tablespoons flour. Add to stew. Cook and stir till thickened and bubbly. Cook and stir 1 minute more. Discard bay leaf. (Return chicken to stew.) Makes 6 servings.

To build a fire for outdoor cooking, follow the tips on this page. Begin by lining the firebox of your grill with foil. Pile charcoal briquettes in a mound, drizzle on liquid charcoal starter, wait one minute, then ignite the coals.

If using a foil drip pan, set it in the bottom of the firebox after the charcoal is ready for cooking. Use a fire rake or long-handled tongs to spread the coals, arranging them around the drip pan.

When grilling steaks, chops, burgers, and other foods that are grilled flat, rake the coals over the entire firebox. Place the coals about ½ inch apart for even heat.

To test the temperature of coals, place your palms just above the coals at cooking level. If you have to remove your hands after 2 seconds, the coals are hot; after 3 seconds, medium-hot; and after 4 seconds, medium.

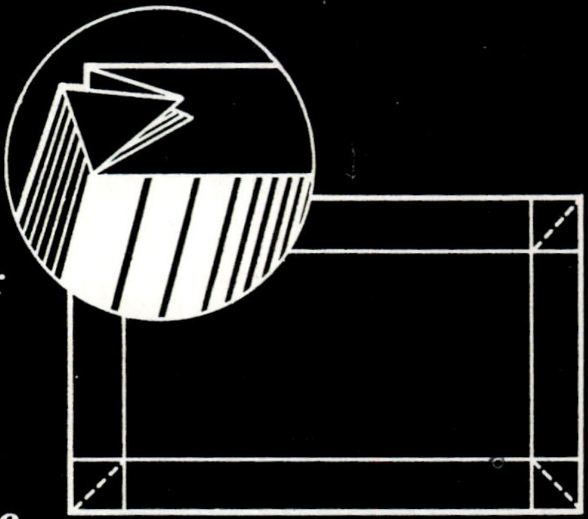

To avoid flare-ups, make a foil drip pan so meat juices and fat drippings fall in the pan rather than on the charcoal. Tear off a piece of 18-inch-wide heavy-duty foil twice the length of your grill and fold it in half for a double thickness. Turn up the edges of the foil 1½ inches. Miter the corners securely and fold tips toward the inside. Set the drip pan under the meat and arrange coals around the pan.

# Orange-Barbecued Chicken

**2 teaspoons cornstarch**
**½ teaspoon chili powder**
**1 8-ounce can tomato sauce**
**¼ cup dark corn syrup**
**¼ cup water**
**2 tablespoons vinegar**
**2 tablespoons orange liqueur**

● For sauce, in a saucepan combine cornstarch and chili powder. Stir in tomato sauce, dark corn syrup, water, and vinegar. Bring mixture to boiling; reduce heat. Simmer, uncovered, 30 minutes. Stir in the orange liqueur. Simmer, uncovered, 5 minutes more; set aside.

**1 2½- to 3-pound whole broiler-fryer chicken**
**Salt**

● Sprinkle chicken cavity with salt. Skewer neck skin to back of chicken. Mount chicken on spit rod (see tip). Attach spit; position drip pan under meat. Place *medium-hot* coals around drip pan. Turn on motor; lower grill hood. Grill over *medium-hot* coals 1½ to 1¾ hours or till tender. Brush chicken often with sauce during the last 10 minutes of grilling. Heat remaining sauce. Pass with chicken. Serves 6 to 8.

**To mount a whole bird for spit roasting, place one holding fork on the spit rod with tines toward the point. Insert the spit rod through the bird lengthwise. Pinch the fork tines together and push into the breast. Tie the wings using 24 inches of cord. Start the cord at the back and loop it around each wing. Wrap cord around the wings again and tie it in center of breast. Loop an 18-inch cord around the tail, then around the legs, and tie tightly. Secure the bird with the second holding fork.**

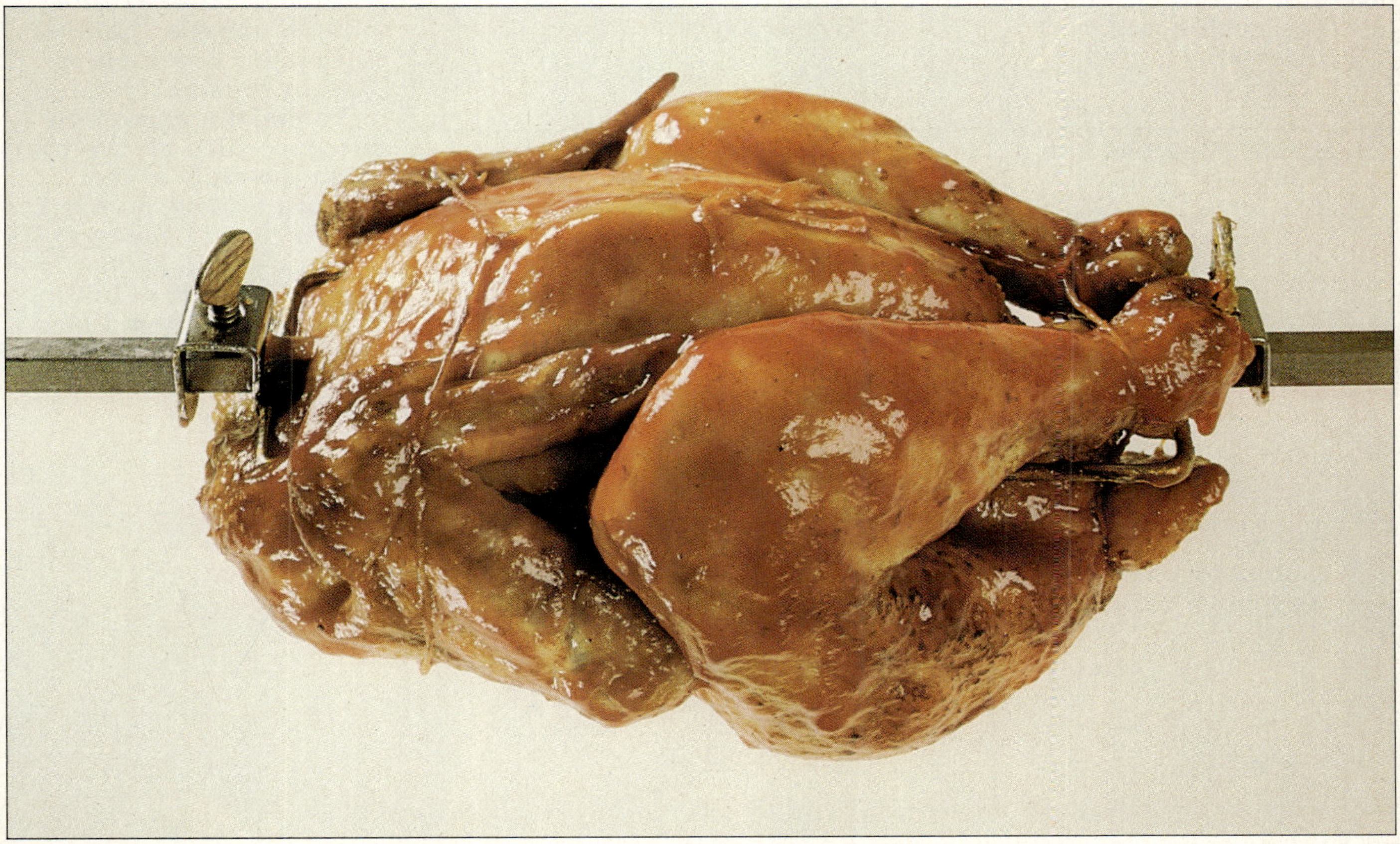

# Beef Alamo

| | |
|---|---|
| **1 pound beef flank steak** | ● To score meat, cut diagonally at 1-inch intervals on both sides, making diamond-shaped cuts. |
| **½ cup hot mustard** | ● Spread mustard on both sides of the steak. Cover; refrigerate several hours. |
| **8 to 12 flour tortillas** | ● Grill steak over *medium-hot* coals 8 to 10 minutes per side. Stack tortillas; wrap in foil. Place on edge of grill to warm. |
| **2 medium tomatoes**<br>**1 medium red onion**<br>**1 4-ounce can green chili peppers, seeded and rinsed** | ● Finely chop tomatoes, red onion, and green chili peppers; stir together. Cut steak into thin slices. Place atop warm tortillas; spoon on tomato mixture. Roll up tortillas. Makes 4 to 6 servings. |

**On the weekend before you enter the stadium for the big football game, pull down the tailgate, set up the grill, and enjoy an on-the-spot picnic. Choose Beef Alamo, a kissing cousin of the enchilada, to headline the menu. Then add a tossed green salad and easy-to-tote brownies.**

# Chinese-Style Chicken

| | |
|---|---|
| **⅔ cup dry sherry**<br>**½ cup sliced green onion**<br>**⅓ cup soy sauce**<br>**¼ cup cooking oil**<br>**2 teaspoons grated gingerroot** | ● For marinade, in a small bowl combine the dry sherry, sliced green onion, soy sauce, cooking oil, and grated gingerroot; mix thoroughly. |
| **4 whole large chicken breasts, split** | ● Place chicken in a plastic bag; set in a deep bowl. Pour marinade over chicken; close bag. Marinate overnight in refrigerator; turn bag occasionally. |
| | ● Drain chicken; reserve marinade. Measure ¼ cup marinade; set aside remaining. Grill chicken over *medium* coals for 20 minutes; brush with some of the ¼ cup marinade. Turn chicken; continue grilling for 20 to 25 minutes or till done, brushing with more marinade. |
| **Water**<br>**1 tablespoon honey**<br>**2 teaspoons cornstarch** | ● Add water to remaining marinade to make 1 cup liquid. In saucepan combine the 1 cup liquid, honey, and cornstarch; cook and stir till thickened and bubbly. Serve over chicken. Makes 8 servings. |

**Chinese-Style Chicken, hot off the grill, is bound to be a success at cookouts. If you like, garnish with fancy green onion fans or brushes.**

**To make green onion brushes, slice off the roots from the ends of the onions; remove all but 2 to 3 inches of the top green portion. Make several slashes at both ends of the onion. Place in ice water to curl back ends.**

# Bacon-Stuffed Jumbo Burger

**4 slices bacon**
**¼ cup finely chopped celery**
**¼ cup chopped onion**
**1 3-ounce can chopped mushrooms, drained**

● In skillet cook bacon till crisp; drain, reserving 2 tablespoons drippings. Crumble bacon; set aside.

Cook celery and onion in reserved drippings till tender. Stir in bacon and mushrooms. Set aside.

**2 beaten eggs**
**¾ cup herb-seasoned stuffing mix**
**2 tablespoons chopped onion**
**2 tablespoons snipped parsley**
**2 tablespoons milk**
**1 tablespoon Worcestershire sauce**
**2 pounds extra-lean ground beef**

● Stir together eggs, stuffing mix, onion, parsley, milk, Worcestershire sauce, ½ teaspoon *salt,* and dash *pepper.*

Add ground beef; mix well. Divide mixture in half.

On sheets of waxed paper, pat each half onto an 8-inch circle. Spoon stuffing over one circle of meat to within 1 inch of edge. Top with second half of meat; peel off top sheet of waxed paper. Seal edges of meat.

**Catsup, warmed**

● Invert burger onto greased wire grill basket; peel off paper. Grill over *medium-hot* coals 15 to 18 minutes. Turn and grill 15 to 18 minutes more or to desired doneness. Cut burger into wedges; serve with catsup. Makes 6 to 8 servings.

**To assemble the burger, spoon stuffing over one circle of meat to within 1 inch of the edge.**

**Top with second half of meat; peel off top sheet of waxed paper. Seal edges of meat. Invert burger onto greased wire grill basket. Peel off paper.**

**A wire grill basket makes it easier to turn the burger. You simply flip the basket.**

# Steak and Bacon Tournedos

*Pictured on the cover—*

**Thinking of giving a small, elegant dinner party? Then consider this recipe for Steak and Bacon Tournedos. Sliced bacon and flecks of parsley are laid atop pounded flank steak. Then it's rolled up jelly roll style and cut into tournedos.**

**1 1- to 1½-pound beef flank steak**
**1 teaspoon garlic salt**
**½ teaspoon pepper**

● Score steak diagonally, making diamond-shaped cuts. Using the fine-toothed side of a meat mallet, pound to about ⅛-inch thickness. Sprinkle steak with garlic salt and pepper.

**4 or 8 slices bacon**

● If desired, precook bacon by heating in a large skillet till just done, but not crisp. Drain.

**2 tablespoons snipped parsley**

● Place bacon slices lengthwise on steak. Sprinkle with snipped parsley. Roll up jelly-roll style, starting at narrow end. Secure meat roll with wooden picks. Cut into 1-inch slices. Secure with decorative skewers if desired. Grill over *medium* coals 15 minutes for medium-rare doneness, turning once.

**1 1¾-ounce envelope hollandaise sauce mix**
**¼ teaspoon dried tarragon, crushed**

● Meanwhile, in a saucepan prepare hollandaise sauce mix according to package directions, adding the tarragon to the dry mix. Serve sauce with the tournedos. Makes 4 servings.

My
Turn to
Cook

# Smoked Pork Chops with Molasses-Orange Sauce

| | | |
|---|---|---|
| **Hickory chips** | ● An hour before cooking, soak about 4 cups hickory chips in enough water to cover; drain. Sprinkle *medium-slow* coals with *half* of the drained chips. | |
| **6 pork loin *or* rib chops, cut 1¼ to 1½ inches thick** | ● Place pork chops on grill. Lower grill hood. Grill, covered, 20 to 25 minutes. | |
| **⅓ cup prepared mustard**<br>**⅓ cup vinegar**<br>**⅓ cup orange marmalade**<br>**¼ cup molasses**<br>**½ teaspoon ground ginger** | ● In saucepan combine mustard, vinegar, marmalade, molasses, and ginger. Cook and stir till marmalade is melted.<br>Brush pork chops with sauce. Turn pork chops and add remaining hickory chips. Grill chops, covered, about 20 minutes more or till done, occasionally brushing with sauce. Makes 6 servings. | |

**If you think there's no way to improve smoke-cooked flavor, try these pork chops. They're thick and juicy and generously brushed with a molasses and orange marmalade sauce. So offer plenty of napkins when you serve them. If you don't have a covered grill, you can make the chops on an uncovered one if you lengthen the cooking time to 30 to 35 minutes on each side.**

## Smoke Cooking

Smoke cooking not only adds an irresistible woodsy flavor to poultry, fish, and meats, it also gives them an appetizing red color. The best wood chips to use for smoke cooking are hickory, oak, hard maple, bay, mahogany, fruit woods, and mesquite. The most common wood, hickory, is available in many supermarkets. Mesquite is available commercially only in the Southwest. Avoid using resinous woods or softwoods such as pine and fir for smoke cooking. The recipes on these two pages are designed for a covered grill like the one pictured at left. You also can prepare the recipes in smoke cooker units, but the cooking times will be substantially longer. Follow the manufacturer's directions for exact times.

# Hickory-Smoked Ribs

**Hickory chips**

- An hour before cooking, soak about 4 cups hickory chips in enough water to cover; drain.

**¾ cup catsup**
**½ cup finely chopped onion**
**¼ cup packed brown sugar**
**3 tablespoons prepared mustard**
**2 tablespoons wine vinegar**
**2 tablespoons Worcestershire sauce**
**1 teaspoon soy sauce**
**½ to ¾ teaspoon bottled hot pepper sauce**
**4 pounds pork loin back ribs *or* spareribs**

- In a saucepan combine the catsup, chopped onion, brown sugar, mustard, wine vinegar, Worcestershire sauce, soy sauce, and bottled hot pepper sauce. Simmer and stir 10 minutes. Set aside.

In a covered grill place *hot* coals on both sides of foil drip pan. Sprinkle with *one-third* of the dampened hickory chips.

Grill ribs about 1 hour or till done. Sprinkle coals with dampened hickory chips every 20 minutes. Brush ribs with catsup mixture during the last 15 minutes of cooking. Pass the remaining catsup mixture. Makes 6 servings.

**Most barbecued rib recipes are best done in a covered grill. To keep the ribs from burning, brush with sauce only during the last 15 minutes of grilling.**

**There are three types of pork ribs. Loin back ribs contain rib bones from the rib area of the loin.**

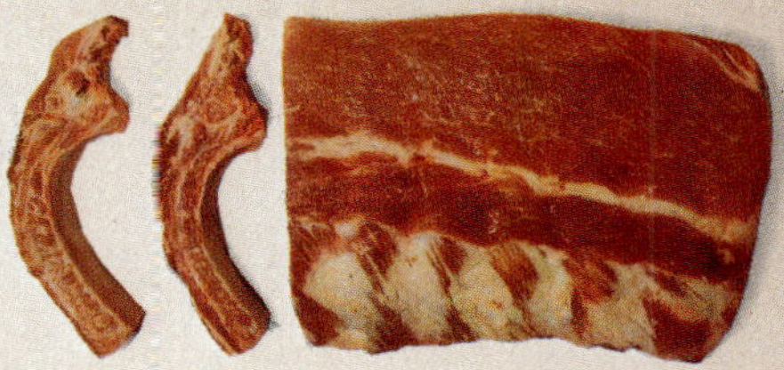

**Spareribs come from the rib cage. Most of the weight is bone with only a thin covering of meat.**

**Loin country-style ribs are the meatiest ribs. They are cut from the shoulder end of back ribs.**

# Smoked Chicken with Potato Stuffing

| | |
|---|---|
| **Hickory chips** | ● An hour before cooking time, soak about 6 cups hickory chips in water. |
| **1 medium potato, peeled and cut up** | ● Cook potato in boiling salted water for 20 minutes or till tender; drain. |
| **1 teaspoon instant chicken bouillon granules**<br>**½ teaspoon dried marjoram, crushed** | ● In a small mixer bowl mash the cooked potato with an electric mixer. Add the bouillon granules, dried marjoram, ¼ cup *water*, and ¼ teaspoon *pepper;* beat till well combined. |
| **2 slices bacon** | ● In a skillet cook bacon till crisp. Drain bacon, reserving drippings in skillet. Crumble bacon; set aside. |
| **¼ cup chopped celery**<br>**¼ cup chopped onion**<br>**1¾ cups whole wheat bread cubes (2 to 2½ slices)**<br>**2 tablespoons snipped parsley** | ● Add celery and onion to the skillet; cook till tender but not brown. Remove from heat; stir in potato mixture, bacon, bread cubes, and parsley.<br>Using a covered grill, arrange *medium-slow* coals at back and sides of firebox. Center a 12x10-inch foil drip pan between coals (see tip for making drip pan, page 24). |
| **1 3- to 4-pound whole roasting chicken *or* three 1¼-pound Cornish game hens**<br>**Cooking oil** | ● Rinse chicken or Cornish game hens; pat dry with paper toweling. Stuff with bread-potato mixture.<br>Skewer neck skin to back of bird or hens; tie legs securely to tail. Twist wing tips under back. Place chicken or hens, breast side up, on grill over drip pan. Brush with cooking oil. Insert meat thermometer in the center of the inside thigh muscle without touching bone.<br>Drain hickory chips. Sprinkle *one-fourth* of the chips over coals. Lower grill hood; grill chicken for 2¼ to 2½ hours (Cornish game hens for 2 to 2¼ hours) or till meat thermometer registers 185° and leg moves easily in socket. Brush chicken or hens often with cooking oil. Add another one-fourth of the hickory chips every 30 minutes. Serves 6. |

**Take your choice of one roasting chicken or three Cornish game hens in this smoke-cooked recipe—both will serve six. Don't pack the stuffing too tightly or it will become firm and compact when cooked. For a tender skin, brush the chicken or hens often with cooking oil.**

**For best results, use only a covered grill for this recipe. You'll get more hickory-smoked flavor, and the covered grill ensures perfect doneness every time.**

# Trout with Orange-Rice Stuffing

**½ cup finely chopped celery**
**3 tablespoons orange juice**
**2 tablespoons finely chopped onion**
**2 tablespoons butter**
**½ teaspoon shredded lemon peel**
**1 tablespoon lemon juice**
**¼ cup long grain rice**

● In a medium saucepan combine the finely chopped celery, orange juice, finely chopped onion, butter, shredded lemon peel, lemon juice, ½ cup *water*, and ½ teaspoon *salt;* bring to boiling. Add long grain rice; cover saucepan.

Reduce heat and simmer the mixture about 20 minutes or till the long grain rice is tender. Remove from heat.

**1 medium orange, sectioned and coarsely chopped**
**¼ cup toasted chopped almonds**

● Add orange pieces and toasted chopped almonds to rice mixture, stirring lightly till combined.

**6 5-ounce fresh *or* frozen pan-dressed trout, heads removed**

● Stuff each fish cavity loosely with about ⅓ cup stuffing. Place fish in a 13x9x2-inch baking dish.

**2 tablespoons cooking oil**

● Brush fish with cooking oil. Cover with foil. Bake in a 350° oven for 30 minutes or till fish flakes easily when tested with a fork. Use 2 large spatulas to transfer fish to serving platter. Serves 6.

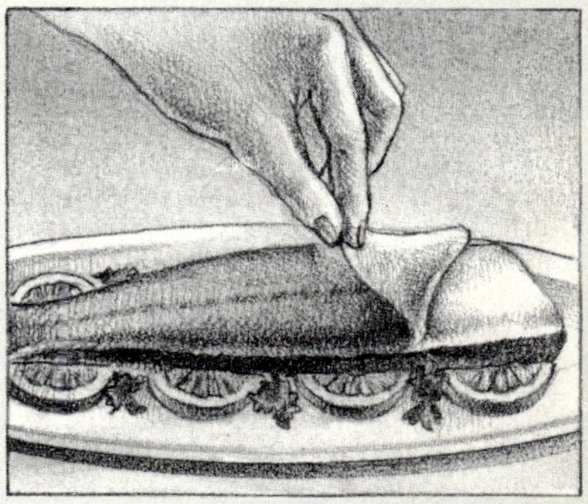

**To serve a cooked fish, begin at the head and cut a ½-inch-deep slit along the back; remove the skin.**

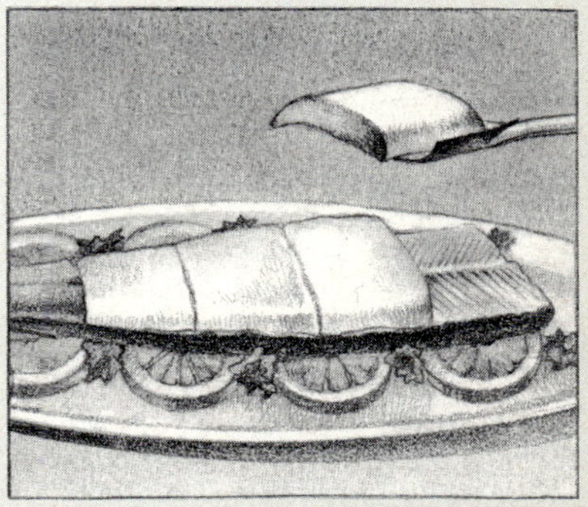

**Without cutting through the backbone, cut the fish into serving-size pieces. Slide a spatula under each piece along the backbone, and carefully lift away from the bones. Turn the fish over and repeat cutting procedure.**

# Salmon Quiche

**1 cup whole wheat flour**
**⅔ cup shredded sharp cheddar cheese**
**¼ cup chopped almonds**
**½ teaspoon salt**
**¼ teaspoon paprika**
**6 tablespoons cooking oil**

● For crust, combine whole wheat flour, the ⅔ cup cheese, almonds, salt, and paprika in a bowl. Stir in oil. Set aside ½ cup of the crust mixture.

Press remaining mixture into the bottom and up the sides of a 9-inch pie plate. Bake crust in a 400° oven for 10 minutes. Remove from oven. Reduce oven temperature to 325°.

**1 15½-ounce can salmon**

● For filling, drain salmon, reserving liquid. Add water to liquid, if necessary, to make ½ cup liquid. Flake salmon, removing bones and skin; set aside.

**3 beaten eggs**
**1 cup dairy sour cream**
**¼ cup mayonnaise *or* salad dressing**
**½ cup shredded sharp cheddar cheese**
**1 tablespoon grated onion**
**¼ teaspoon dried dillweed**
**3 drops bottled hot pepper sauce**

● In a bowl combine eggs, sour cream, mayonnaise or salad dressing, and reserved salmon liquid. Stir in salmon, the ½ cup cheese, grated onion, dillweed, and hot pepper sauce.

Spoon filling into the prebaked crust. Sprinkle with reserved crust mixture. Bake in the 325° oven for 45 minutes or till a knife inserted near center comes out clean. Makes 6 servings.

**To prepare the crust for Salmon Quiche, use your hands to spread the crust mixture across the pie plate in an even layer. Pat the mixture firmly onto the sides and bottom of the pie plate to form an even crust. Make sure the sides and bottom are the same thickness.**

**Baking the crust before filling it makes the crust crispier, and the finished quiche easier to serve.**

# Baked Fish Amandine

**1 pound frozen fish fillets**

● Thaw fish; pat dry with paper toweling. (Or, micro-thaw, covered, on HIGH about 2 minutes or till fillets are pliable on the outside, but still icy in the center.) Cut fish crosswise into four pieces.

**Salt**
**White pepper**

● Place fish in a 10x6x2-inch baking dish; sprinkle with salt and pepper.

**1 teaspoon shredded lemon peel**
**2 tablespoons lemon juice**
**¼ cup butter *or* margarine, melted**

● Stir together the lemon peel, lemon juice, and *half* of the melted butter or margarine; pour over fish in baking dish. Bake, covered, in a 400° oven for 20 minutes; remove from oven. Pour remaining butter or margarine over fish.

**1 4-ounce can sliced mushrooms, drained**
**¼ cup toasted sliced almonds**
**2 tablespoons snipped parsley**

● Top with drained sliced mushrooms, sliced almonds, and snipped parsley.

Return fish to oven; bake, uncovered, 10 to 15 minutes more or till fish flakes easily when tested with a fork. Serves 4.

**MICROWAVE TIMING**
Prepare fish as directed at left. Pour lemon juice mixture over fish in baking dish. Micro-cook, covered, on HIGH about 6 minutes, rotating dish once. Add the remaining butter, mushrooms, sliced almonds, and snipped parsley. Micro-cook, covered, 2 to 4 minutes more or till fish flakes easily when tested with a fork.

# Glazed Creole Shrimp

| | |
|---|---|
| **¼ cup chopped onion**<br>**1 clove garlic, minced**<br>**1 tablespoon butter** | ● To make sauce, in a saucepan cook the chopped onion and minced garlic in butter till tender but not brown. |
| **¼ cup chopped celery**<br>**¼ cup chopped green pepper**<br>**⅛ to ¼ teaspoon ground red pepper**<br>**1 bay leaf**<br>**1 8-ounce can tomato sauce**<br>**¼ cup catsup**<br>**3 tablespoons dry white wine** | ● Add chopped celery, chopped green pepper, ground red pepper, bay leaf, ¼ teaspoon *salt*, and a dash *pepper*.<br>Stir in the tomato sauce, catsup, and *1 tablespoon* of the dry white wine. Simmer, covered, for 20 to 25 minutes. Remove bay leaf from tomato sauce. |
| **2 tablespoons butter**<br>**2 tablespoons light molasses**<br>**2 tablespoons prepared mustard**<br>**1 tablespoon Worcestershire sauce** | ● Meanwhile, in a medium skillet melt the 2 tablespoons butter. Add the remaining 2 tablespoons dry white wine, the light molasses, prepared mustard, and Worcestershire sauce. Bring to boiling; reduce heat to medium-high. |
| **1 pound large fresh *or* frozen shrimp, peeled and deveined**<br>**2 cups hot cooked rice** | ● Add shrimp to skillet; cook and stir over medium-high heat 3 to 5 minutes.<br>Pour sauce over rice. Top sauce with shrimp mixture. Makes 4 servings. |

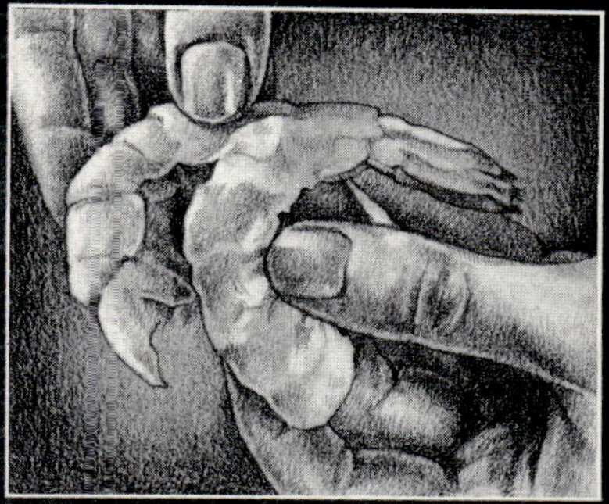

**To clean shrimp, remove the shell from the head, leaving the tail section intact.**

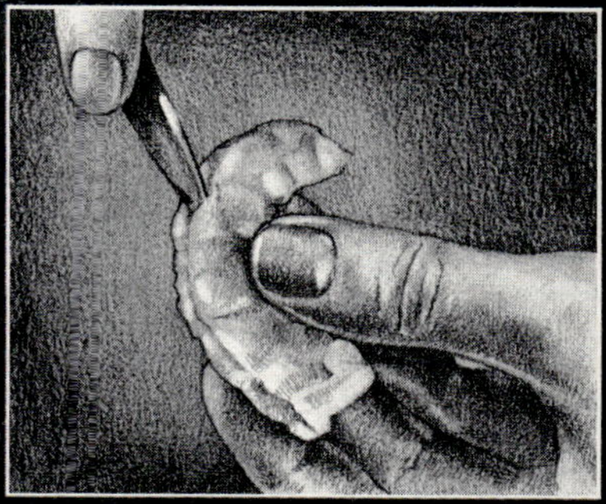

**To devein shrimp, slit the back of the shrimp and scrape out the black vein with the tip of a knife.**

# Oriental Flair

If you're looking for a new way to serve roasted whole game birds such as duck, goose, or pheasant, try carving them with an authentic Oriental flair. These directions will tell you how. Place the roasted bird breast-side up; cut it in half lengthwise through the breast using a sharp knife or cleaver. Cut off the wings and legs close to the body; set aside. Cut off the backbone on each half of the bird. Cut each part of the backbone into bite-size pieces and reassemble on a serving platter. Cut the wings and legs into two or three pieces and arrange them on each side of the backbone. Carefully chop the remaining bird into bite-size pieces. Reassemble each half into its original shape as shown in the drawing above.

# Duck with Ginger-Fruit Sauce

| | |
|---|---|
| **1 4- to 5-pound domestic duck *or* two 1½- to 2-pound wild ducks, quartered** | ● Cut bird or birds into quarters. Place pieces on a rack in shallow roasting pan. Cover with foil; bake in a 375° oven for 1¼ hours for domestic duck (45 minutes for wild ducks) or till almost done. Remove fat as necessary. |
| **Ginger-Fruit Sauce**<br>**2 tablespoons hoisin sauce**<br>**1 tablespoon dry sherry**<br>**1 tablespoon orange juice** | ● In a small mixing bowl combine *half* of the Ginger-Fruit Sauce, the hoisin sauce, dry sherry, and orange juice. Brush duck pieces with mixture. |
| **3 tablespoons sliced green onion**<br>**Orange slices (optional)** | ● Bake, uncovered, 10 minutes more or till glazed. Sprinkle with sliced green onion. Garnish with orange slices, if desired. Serve with the remaining Ginger-Fruit Sauce. Makes 4 servings. |

**Ginger-Fruit Sauce**: In a small saucepan combine ½ cup *applesauce;* ¼ cup *vinegar;* ¼ cup packed *brown sugar;* ¼ cup *peach preserves;* 1½ teaspoons grated *ginger-root;* 1 small clove *garlic,* minced; and several dashes *ground red pepper.* Cook and stir till mixture boils. Reduce heat; simmer, uncovered, 10 minutes. Makes about 1 cup.

**Hoisin sauce, available in Oriental food stores, adds a distinct Chinese flavor to this recipe.**

# German-Style Rabbit

- **¼ cup all-purpose flour**
- **½ teaspoon salt**
- **¼ teaspoon pepper**
- **1 2- to 2½-pound rabbit, cut up**

● Combine the all-purpose flour, ½ teaspoon salt, and pepper in a plastic bag. Add 2 or 3 rabbit pieces at a time and shake to coat.

- **2 tablespoons cooking oil**

● In a large skillet brown rabbit in hot cooking oil about 10 minutes, turning to brown evenly.

- **2 tablespoons brown sugar**
- **2 tablespoons vinegar**
- **1 teaspoon minced dried onion**

● Combine brown sugar, vinegar, minced dried onion, and ¾ cup *water*. Pour over rabbit in skillet. Cover and cook over low heat for 25 minutes. Remove rabbit from skillet.

- **8 cups shredded cabbage**
- **2 medium apples, cored and chopped**
- **1 teaspoon caraway seed**
- **½ teaspoon salt**

● Stir cabbage, apples, caraway seed, and ½ teaspoon salt into skillet. Return rabbit to skillet. Cover and cook 20 minutes more or till rabbit is done and cabbage is tender. Makes 4 servings.

**A domestic rabbit or freshly bagged wild rabbit is suitable for this recipe. But remember, wild rabbit is generally tougher and may require longer cooking than domestic rabbit.**

# Burgundy-Basted Pheasant

- **1 2- to 2¼-pound pheasant, quartered**
- **1 small onion, sliced and separated into rings**
- **⅓ cup burgundy**
- **¼ cup lemon juice**
- **3 tablespoons cooking oil**
- **1 tablespoon Worcestershire sauce**
- **1 clove garlic, minced**
- **1 teaspoon dried marjoram, crushed**
- **½ teaspoon salt**
- **¼ teaspoon bottled hot pepper sauce**
- **⅛ teaspoon pepper**

● Place pheasant and onion rings in a large plastic bag; set in a deep bowl.

To make marinade, combine the remaining ingredients. Pour marinade over pheasant and onion. Close the bag. Marinate several hours or overnight in refrigerator, turning pheasant occasionally.

Drain the pheasant and onion rings, reserving ¼ cup of the marinade. Place pheasant, onion, and the reserved marinade in a 2-quart casserole. Cover and bake in a 350° oven for 1 to 1¼ hours or till done, spooning pan juices over pheasant occasionally. Makes 2 servings.

**This recipe is especially good if you happen to bag an older bird. The marinade adds flavor, and moist-heat cooking contributes tenderness.**

# Venison Stew

**1 cup apple juice**
**⅓ cup cider vinegar**
**1 medium onion, sliced**
**6 whole cloves**
**1 bay leaf**

● To make marinade, in a medium saucepan combine the apple juice, vinegar, onion, cloves, and bay leaf. Bring to boiling. Reduce heat; simmer, covered, 10 minutes. Cool.

**1 1-pound boneless venison *or* beef round steak, cut into 1-inch cubes**
**¼ cup all-purpose flour**
**1½ teaspoons salt**
**¼ teaspoon pepper**
**⅛ teaspoon dry mustard**

● Place meat in a large plastic bag. Pour marinade over meat. Close the bag. Marinate meat in the refrigerator overnight, turning occasionally.

Drain meat, reserving marinade and onion; discard cloves and bay leaf. Pat meat dry with paper toweling. Combine flour, salt, pepper, and dry mustard. Coat meat with flour mixture.

**2 tablespoons cooking oil**
**2 teaspoons Worcestershire sauce**
**2 carrots, cut into ¾-inch slices**
**1 potato, peeled and cut into 1-inch cubes**
**2 stalks celery, sliced into 1-inch pieces**

● In a large saucepan brown meat, half at a time, in hot oil. Add water to the reserved marinade to make 2 cups liquid. Add to meat in saucepan along with the reserved sliced onion and Worcestershire sauce. Bring to boiling. Reduce heat; cover and simmer 1 hour. Stir in carrots, potato, and celery. Cover; simmer for 45 to 60 minutes more or till meat and vegetables are tender. Makes 4 servings.

**If you aren't a hunter, venison might be hard to locate. But when you find it, you'll agree that this recipe is worth the search. (Try beef as a stand-in.) Marinating complements the flavor of venison and helps reduce any gamey taste.**

## Hunter's Roasting Chart

| Game Birds | Weight | Oven Temp. | Roasting Time | Servings | Special Instructions |
|---|---|---|---|---|---|
| **Wild Duck** | 1½-2 lbs. | 400° | 1-1½ hrs. | Two | Stuff loosely with quartered onions and apples; discard after roasting, if desired. Do not rub with oil. |
| **Wild Goose** | 2-4 lbs.<br>4-6 lbs. | 400° | 1½-2 hrs.<br>2-3 hrs. | Two<br>Four | Stuff loosely with quartered onions and apples; discard after roasting, if desired. Baste often. |
| **Pheasant** | 2-3 lbs. | 350° | 1½-2½ hrs. | Two or Three | Place bacon slices over breast. |
| **Quail** | 4-6 oz. | 400° | 30-45 min. | One-half | Place bacon slices over breast. |
| **Domestic Duck** | 3-5 lbs. | 375° | 1½-2¼ hrs. | Three or Four | Prick skin to allow fat to escape. During roasting, spoon off fat. |
| **Domestic Goose** | 7-9 lbs.<br>9-11 lbs. | 350° | 2½-3 hrs.<br>3-3½ hrs. | Six<br>Eight | Prick skin to allow fat to escape. During roasting, spoon off fat. |

# Four-Cheese Lasagna

| | |
|---|---|
| **6 ounces lasagna noodles** | ● In a large saucepan cook lasagna noodles according to package directions; drain. Set aside. |
| **½ pound ground beef**<br>**½ cup chopped onion**<br>**⅓ cup chopped celery**<br>**1 clove garlic, minced** | ● In a large skillet cook ground beef, chopped onion, celery, and minced garlic till meat is brown and vegetables are tender. Drain off fat. |
| **1½ teaspoons dried basil, crushed**<br>**¼ teaspoon dried oregano, crushed**<br>**1 3-ounce package cream cheese, cubed**<br>**⅓ cup light cream *or* milk** | ● Stir in the dried basil, dried oregano, ¼ teaspoon *salt*, and ⅛ teaspoon *pepper*. Add the cream cheese and light cream or milk. Cook and stir over low heat till cheese is melted. |
| **½ cup dry white wine**<br>**½ cup shredded cheddar *or* gouda cheese (2 ounces)** | ● Stir in dry white wine. Gradually add the shredded cheddar or gouda cheese. Cook and stir till cheese is nearly melted; remove from heat. |
| **1 cup cream-style cottage cheese**<br>**1 slightly beaten egg** | ● In small bowl stir together the cream-style cottage cheese and the slightly beaten egg. |
| **6 ounces sliced mozzarella cheese** | ● Layer *half* of the cooked noodles in a greased 10x6x2-inch baking dish. Top with *half* of the meat sauce, *half* of the cottage cheese mixture, and *half* of the mozzarella cheese. Repeat layers.<br>Bake, uncovered, in a 375° oven for 30 to 35 minutes. Let stand 10 minutes before serving. Makes 6 servings. |

**The man who sent us this recipe got the idea while he was in Spain. Luckily for us, he was so impressed with Spanish all-white lasagna that he developed his own Four-Cheese Lasagna, a main dish boasting cream, cheddar, cottage, and mozzarella cheeses.**

**MICROWAVE TIMING**
Micro-cook, uncovered, on HIGH for 10 to 12 minutes, turning dish once.

# Estofado

Estofado is a main-dish stew that owes its flavor to raisins, dried apricots, dry red wine, and a little bundle of herbs called a Bouquet Garni.

**1 pound pork stew meat, cut into 1-inch cubes**
**1 tablespoon cooking oil**
**1 cup dry red wine**
**1 8-ounce can (1 cup) tomatoes, cut up**
**1 large onion, cut into ¼-inch-thick slices**
**¼ cup raisins**
**¼ cup dried apricots, halved**
**1 clove garlic, minced**

● In a large saucepan or Dutch oven brown the 1-inch pork cubes in the hot cooking oil.

Add the dry red wine, *undrained* tomatoes, onion slices, raisins, dried apricots, minced garlic, ½ cup *water*, 1 teaspoon *salt*, and ⅛ teaspoon *pepper*.

**Bouquet Garni (see recipe below)**

● Add Bouquet Garni to meat mixture. Simmer, covered, 1 hour.

**1 green pepper, cut into strips**
**½ cup sliced fresh mushrooms**
**¼ cup sliced pitted ripe olives**

● Add green pepper strips, sliced mushrooms, and sliced ripe olives; simmer 20 minutes more. Remove and discard Bouquet Garni.

**½ cup cold water**
**1 tablespoon all-purpose flour**
**Hot cooked rice**

● Combine cold water and all-purpose flour; stir into meat mixture. Cook and stir till thickened and bubbly. Cook and stir 1 minute more. Serve over rice. Makes 6 servings.

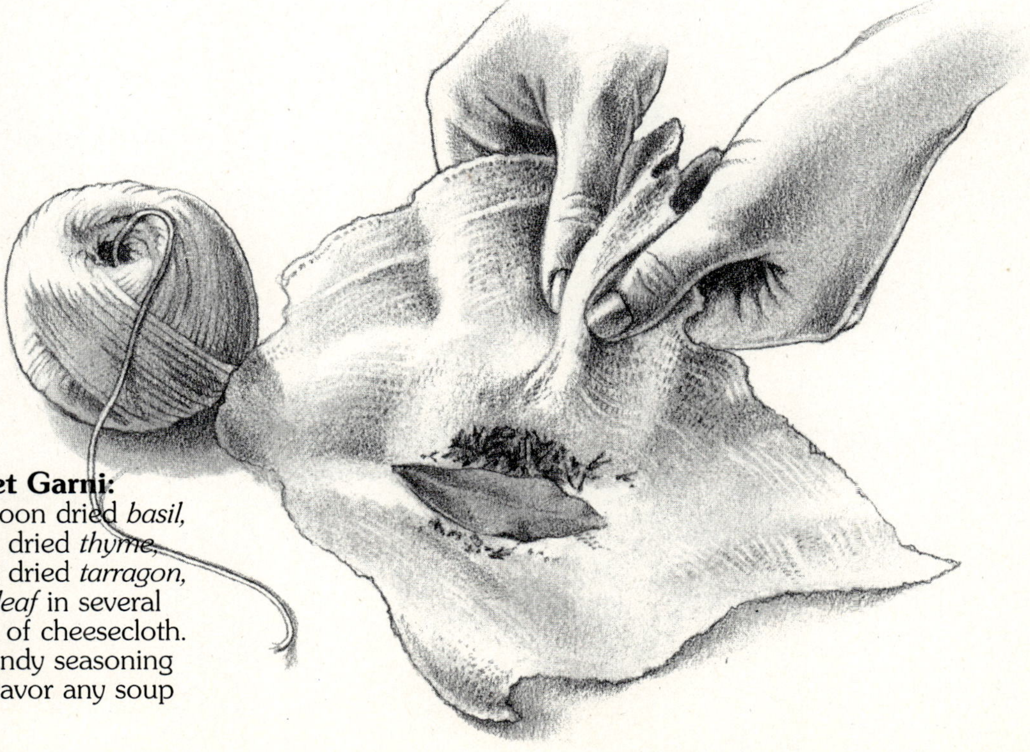

● **Bouquet Garni:** Tie 1 teaspoon dried *basil,* 1 teaspoon dried *thyme,* 1 teaspoon dried *tarragon,* and 1 *bay leaf* in several thicknesses of cheesecloth. Use this handy seasoning packet to flavor any soup or stew.

# Beer-Baked Chicken

| | |
|---|---|
| **1 medium onion, chopped**<br>**2 tablespoons butter *or* margarine** | ● For the sauce, in a saucepan cook the chopped onion in butter or margarine till tender but not brown. |
| **1 10¾-ounce can condensed tomato soup**<br>**⅔ cup beer**<br>**1 teaspoon curry powder**<br>**½ teaspoon dried oregano, crushed**<br>**Dash pepper** | ● Stir in the tomato soup, beer, curry powder, dried oregano, and pepper. Simmer, uncovered, for 10 minutes. |
| **3 whole medium chicken breasts (2¼ pounds)** | ● Skin chicken breasts and halve (see tip right). Arrange in a 12x7½x2-inch baking dish. Pour sauce over chicken. Bake, uncovered, in a 350° oven for 50 to 55 minutes or till done. |
| **¼ cup grated Parmesan cheese** | ● Transfer chicken to a serving platter. Sprinkle Parmesan cheese atop chicken. Skim fat from sauce; pass the sauce with chicken. Makes 6 servings. |

**There are two easy ways to halve a chicken breast. One way is to divide the chicken breast into two lengthwise pieces by cutting along the breastbone. The other way is to divide the chicken breast crosswise by grasping and bending the breast between the wishbone and breastbone and cutting between the bones.**

**MICROWAVE TIMING**
Micro-cook, covered, on HIGH, about 20 minutes or till chicken is tender, rearranging pieces and spooning the sauce over after 10 and 15 minutes.

# Vegetables in Beer Batter

| | |
|---|---|
| **1⅓ cups all-purpose flour**<br>**2 tablespoons grated Parmesan cheese**<br>**1 tablespoon snipped parsley**<br>**1 teaspoon salt**<br>**Dash garlic powder** | ● In a large mixer bowl combine the all-purpose flour, grated Parmesan cheese, snipped parsley, salt, and garlic powder. |
| **2 egg yolks**<br>**1 12-ounce can beer**<br>**1 tablespoon olive *or* cooking oil** | ● Stir in egg yolks, beer, and olive or cooking oil; beat on low speed of electric mixer till smooth. |
| **2 egg whites** | ● Wash beaters thoroughly. In a small mixer bowl beat the egg whites till stiff peaks form (peaks stand straight). Fold into beer batter. |
| **Green pepper strips, sliced mild green chili peppers, cauliflower flowerets, broccoli buds, whole mushrooms, *or* parsley sprigs**<br>**Cooking oil for deep-fat frying** | ● Pat green pepper strips, chili pepper slices, cauliflower flowerets, broccoli buds, mushrooms, or parsley sprigs dry with paper toweling; dip in beer batter. Fry in deep hot oil (375°), a few pieces at a time, for 2 to 5 minutes or till vegetables are golden.<br>Drain on paper toweling. (Keep fried vegetables warm in a 300° oven while deep-frying the remaining vegetables.) Makes about 3½ cups batter. |

**To know when egg whites are stiffly beaten, turn off the electric mixer and lift up the beaters. Stiffly beaten egg whites will stand in straight peaks.**

# Sherry-Garlic Shrimp

**1 pound fresh *or* frozen shrimp, peeled and deveined**
**1 12-ounce can beer**
**1 cup bias-sliced celery**
**2 tablespoons sliced green onion**

● In a large saucepan combine the shrimp, beer, bias-sliced celery, and sliced green onion; bring to boiling.

Reduce heat; simmer 1 minute or till shrimp turn pink. Drain.

**¼ cup butter *or* margarine**
**2 tablespoons dry sherry**
**¼ teaspoon garlic salt**
**¼ teaspoon dried fines herbes, crushed**

● Meanwhile, in a small saucepan melt the butter or margarine. Stir in dry sherry, garlic salt, and fines herbes. Heat through; toss with drained shrimp mixture. Makes 8 appetizer servings.

**Sherry-Garlic Shrimp offers a bonus. It's an appetizer featuring two spirits. The shrimp are cooked in beer, then served with butter that is spiked with sherry.**

# Sole Caledonia

**½ cup dry white wine**
**1 pound fresh *or* frozen sole fillets**

● In a skillet bring the ½ cup wine to boiling. Add fillets; simmer, covered, 2 to 3 minutes (4 to 8 minutes for frozen fillets) or till fish flakes easily when tested with a fork. (Or, arrange fillets in a 10x6x2-inch baking dish. Add wine. Micro-cook, covered, on HIGH about 4 to 6 minutes or till fish flakes easily when tested with a fork.)

**The man who sent us this recipe grew up in Scotland where one of his favorite dishes was sole topped with home-style vegetables. Later, he improved the old standby and came up with elegant Sole Caledonia.**

**½ of a 10-ounce package frozen cut asparagus, cooked and drained**
**½ cup halved cherry tomatoes**

● Drain fillets and arrange in a 10x6x2-inch baking dish; season with a little salt. Top with asparagus and cherry tomatoes.

**½ cup sliced mushrooms**
**2 tablespoons butter**
**2 tablespoons all-purpose flour**
**Dash white pepper**
**1¼ cups milk**

● In a small saucepan cook mushrooms in 2 tablespoons butter till tender. Stir in flour, ½ teaspoon *salt,* and white pepper. Stir in milk; cook and stir till thickened and bubbly.

**1 slightly beaten egg yolk**
**¼ cup dry white wine**

● Gradually stir ½ cup hot mixture into egg yolk. Return all to saucepan; cook and stir till mixture bubbles. Remove from heat; stir in the ¼ cup wine. Pour over fillets and vegetables.

**1 cup soft bread crumbs**
**¼ cup grated Parmesan cheese**
**2 tablespoons butter, melted**

● Combine bread crumbs, Parmesan cheese, and 2 tablespoons melted butter. Sprinkle evenly over all. Bake, uncovered, in a 350° oven for 20 to 25 minutes or till heated through. Makes 4 servings.

**MICROWAVE TIMING**
Micro-cook, covered with waxed paper, on HIGH about 6 minutes or till warm, turning dish once.

# Skillet Potato Breakfast

| | |
|---|---|
| **6 slices bacon** | ● In a 10-inch skillet cook bacon till crisp. Drain; reserve 2 tablespoons drippings in skillet. Set bacon aside. |
| **3 cups frozen hash brown potatoes with onions and peppers**<br>**1 cup shredded Monterey Jack *or* pepper cheese** | ● Cook frozen hash brown potatoes in reserved drippings till golden. Crumble 2 slices of the bacon; stir into potatoes. Sprinkle shredded cheese atop potatoes. Place remaining 4 slices of bacon in an X atop cheese. |
| **4 eggs** | ● Carefully break 1 egg into each triangle formed by bacon. Cover; cook over medium heat about 6 minutes or till eggs are set. Makes 4 servings. |

**The beauty of this recipe is that it takes only four ingredients and a frying pan. The man who sent it to us says it's great for camping trips.**

# Breakfast Pizza

| | |
|---|---|
| **1 pound bulk pork sausage** | ● In a skillet cook the sausage till brown; drain off fat. |
| **1 package (8) refrigerated crescent rolls** | ● Separate crescent roll dough into 8 triangles. Place in an ungreased 12-inch pizza pan, with points toward the center. Press over bottom and up sides to form a crust; seal perforations. |
| **1 cup frozen loose-pack hash brown potatoes, thawed**<br>**1 cup shredded sharp cheddar cheese** | ● Spoon cooked sausage over crust. Sprinkle with thawed hash brown potatoes. Top with shredded cheddar cheese. |
| **5 eggs**<br>**¼ cup milk** | ● In bowl beat together eggs, milk, ½ teaspoon *salt,* and ⅛ teaspoon *pepper.* Pour into crust. |
| **2 tablespoons grated Parmesan cheese** | ● Sprinkle Parmesan cheese over all. Bake in a 375° oven for 25 to 30 minutes. Makes 6 to 8 servings. |

**The cook who invented this recipe says, "I've startled a few guests when I've told them we're having pizza for breakfast. But they're delighted when I bring out this version. It's an easy way to serve eggs, sausage, hash brown potatoes, and rolls all at once. And my children like it too, even though they usually won't touch eggs for breakfast."**

# Brunch Egg Casserole

The next time you're making breakfast for a crowd, try Brunch Egg Casserole. You can serve 10 hungry people bacon and eggs out of one dish. Add a fruit cup, sweet rolls or muffins, and milk or coffee for a menu that will bring rave reviews.

**8 slices bacon**
**4 cups plain croutons**
**2 cups shredded cheddar cheese (8 ounces)**

● Preheat oven to 325°. In a skillet cook bacon till crisp; drain and crumble. Spread plain croutons in bottom of a 13x9x2-inch baking dish. Sprinkle cheese and bacon atop croutons.

**8 slightly beaten eggs**
**4 cups milk**
**½ teaspoon salt**
**½ teaspoon onion salt**
**⅛ teaspoon pepper**

● Combine the eggs, milk, salt, onion salt, and pepper; pour over cheese and bacon. Bake in the 325° oven 40 to 45 minutes or till knife inserted near center comes out clean. Let stand 5 minutes before serving. Makes 10 servings.

# Sausage Brunch Cake

Do you avoid making pancakes because you end up slaving over the griddle while everyone else eats? With Sausage-Brunch Cake you can mix up the batter, top it with brown-and-serve sausages, and let it bake. There's no last-minute hassle. When it's time to serve, top the cake with our homemade pineapple sauce or maple-flavored syrup.

**1 slightly beaten egg**
**¾ cup milk**
**2 tablespoons butter *or* margarine, melted**

● Preheat oven to 400°. In mixing bowl combine slightly beaten egg, milk, and melted butter or margarine.

**1 cup all-purpose flour**
**1 tablespoon sugar**
**2 teaspoons baking powder**
**¼ teaspoon salt**
**¼ teaspoon ground nutmeg**

● In a small bowl stir together the all-purpose flour, 1 tablespoon sugar, baking powder, salt, and ground nutmeg. Stir egg mixture into dry ingredients just till moistened.

**1 8-ounce package brown-and-serve sausage links**

● Spread batter into a greased 10x6x2-inch baking dish. Arrange brown-and-serve sausages atop.

**1 tablespoon sugar**
**¼ teaspoon ground cinnamon**

● Mix 1 tablespoon sugar and cinnamon. Sprinkle atop batter. Bake in the 400° oven for 18 to 20 minutes or till brunch cake is done.

**1 8-ounce can crushed pineapple (juice pack)**
**½ cup maple-flavored syrup**
**2 teaspoons cornstarch**
**½ teaspoon lemon juice**

● Meanwhile, for pineapple sauce, in a saucepan combine the *undrained* pineapple, maple-flavored syrup, cornstarch, and lemon juice. Cook and stir till mixture is thickened and bubbly. Cook and stir 2 minutes more; remove from heat.

● Cut cake into 6 pieces. Serve with pineapple sauce. Makes 6 servings.

# Canadian Bacon-Filled Gougère

| | |
|---|---|
| Butter<br>1 cup water<br>6 tablespoons butter<br>½ teaspoon salt<br>Dash pepper<br>1 cup all-purpose flour | ● Butter a 12x7½x2-inch baking dish. In saucepan combine water, the 6 tablespoons butter, salt, and pepper; bring to boiling. Add flour; cook and stir over medium heat till mixture forms a ball that doesn't separate. Remove from heat. |
| 4 eggs<br>2 cups shredded mozzarella cheese (8 ounces) | ● Cool 5 minutes. Add eggs, one at a time, beating by hand after each addition till smooth. Stir in *1¾ cups* of the cheese. Spread mixture over the bottom and up the sides of baking dish. Bake in a 400° oven 20 minutes. |
| 1 tablespoon butter<br>2 cups sliced fresh mushrooms<br>¼ cup sliced green onion | ● Meanwhile, in a saucepan melt the 1 tablespoon butter. Add the sliced mushrooms and green onion. Cook and stir till mushrooms are tender. |
| 1 tablespoon cornstarch<br>1 8-ounce can tomatoes, drained and cut up<br>2 tablespoons dry white wine<br>2 tablespoons catsup<br>½ teaspoon Worcestershire sauce<br>2 cups Canadian-style bacon cut into bite-size strips | ● Stir in cornstarch. Add tomatoes, dry white wine, catsup, and Worcestershire sauce. Cook and stir till mixture is thickened and bubbly. Cook and stir 1 minute more. Stir in Canadian-style bacon.<br>Pour mixture into partially baked crust; sprinkle with the remaining cheese. Bake 15 to 20 minutes more or till puffed and golden. Makes 6 servings. |

**Once the flour is mixed into the liquid, cook and stir till the mixture forms a smooth ball.**

**After the second egg has been added, the mixture will separate into clumps. Continue adding one egg at a time, beating till the mixture is smooth.**

# Basic Omelets

**6 eggs**
**3 tablespoons water**
**$\frac{1}{4}$ teaspoon salt**

● In a bowl beat together the eggs, water, salt, and $\frac{1}{8}$ teaspoon *pepper* with a fork till well combined and frothy.

**2 tablespoons butter *or* margarine**
**Sausage-Sprout Filling *or* Peaches and Cream Filling**

● In a 10-inch skillet with flared sides, heat *half* of the butter till it sizzles. Lift and tilt pan to coat sides. Add *half* of egg mixture; cook over medium heat (see tip, right).

When eggs are set, remove from heat. Spoon *half* of the desired filling across center. Fold $\frac{1}{3}$ of omelet over center; overlap remaining $\frac{1}{3}$ atop. Transfer to plate. Keep warm. Repeat with the remaining egg mixture. Serves 2 or 4.

**Sausage-Sprout Filling:** Slice one 8-ounce package *brown and serve sausages.* In skillet cook sausage just till it begins to brown. Add $\frac{1}{2}$ cup chopped *green pepper.* Cook and stir till sausage is brown and green pepper is tender. Stir in 1 cup fresh *bean sprouts.* Keep warm.

**Peaches and Cream Filling:** Drain and cut up one $8\frac{3}{4}$-ounce can *sliced peaches.* Mix $\frac{1}{2}$ cup dairy *sour cream,* 2 tablespoons *brown sugar,* and $\frac{1}{8}$ teaspoon *ground cinnamon.* Fold in fruit.

**Run a metal spatula around the edge of the skillet, lifting the eggs to allow the uncooked portion to flow underneath. Tip the pan to help the uncooked egg flow easier.**

**Spread half of the Sausage-Sprout Filling across the center of the omelet. Then use the spatula to fold a third of the omelet over the filling.**

# Shrimp Omelets

**1 tablespoon butter**
**1 tablespoon all-purpose flour**
**$\frac{1}{2}$ cup milk**
**$\frac{1}{4}$ teaspoon dried dillweed**

● In small saucepan melt butter. Stir in flour till blended. Add milk and dillweed all at once. Cook and stir over medium heat till mixture is thickened and bubbly. Cook and stir 1 minute more.

**$\frac{1}{2}$ cup shredded Swiss cheese (2 ounces)**
**1 $4\frac{1}{2}$-ounce can shrimp, rinsed and drained**
**$\frac{1}{4}$ cup dairy sour cream**
**1 tablespoon dry sherry**

● Over low heat stir in cheese till melted. Stir in shrimp, sour cream, and dry sherry. Cook and stir till heated through. (Do not boil.) Cover and keep warm.

**Basic Omelets**
**Snipped parsley**

● Prepare Basic Omelets. Fill *each* omelet with $\frac{1}{2}$ cup of the shrimp mixture. Spoon the remaining mixture atop; sprinkle with parsley. Serves 2 or 4.

**Overlap the remaining third atop filling. Transfer the omelet to a plate.**

# Whole Wheat Mix for Pancakes and Waffles

**8 cups all-purpose flour**
**2 cups whole wheat flour**
**⅓ cup baking powder**
**¼ cup sugar**
**2 teaspoons salt**
**2 teaspoons ground cinnamon**

● In a large bowl combine the all-purpose flour, whole wheat flour, baking powder, sugar, salt, and cinnamon.

Store mix in a covered container up to six weeks. Makes about 11 cups mix.

**Store this handy pancake and waffle mix on the shelf. The recipe makes enough for 5 delicious batches of pancakes or waffles.**

● *For 8 (4-inch) pancakes:* In a bowl beat 1 *egg* slightly. Add 1 cup *milk* and ⅓ cup *cooking oil.* Stir into 2 cups *Whole Wheat Mix;* beat till smooth. Bake on a hot, lightly greased griddle using about ¼ cup batter for each pancake.

● *For 8 (4-inch) waffles:* In a bowl beat 2 *eggs* slightly. Add 1⅓ cups *milk* and ½ cup *cooking oil.* Stir into 2 cups *Whole Wheat Mix;* beat till smooth. Bake on a hot, lightly greased waffle iron using about ¼ cup batter for each waffle.

# Cheese and Bacon Waffles

**6 slices bacon**

● In a skillet cook bacon till crisp. Drain and crumble bacon.

**2 beaten eggs**
**1 cup milk**
**½ cup cooking oil**
**2 cups Whole Wheat Mix *or* packaged pancake mix**

● In a bowl combine the beaten eggs, milk, and cooking oil.

Place the Whole Wheat Mix or packaged pancake mix in a bowl. Add egg mixture; beat till smooth.

**1 cup shredded cheddar cheese (4 ounces)**

● Fold in cheese and *three-quarters* of the crumbled bacon. Bake on a hot, lightly greased waffle iron, using about ¼ cup batter for each waffle.

**Maple-flavored syrup**

● Top each serving with maple-flavored syrup and some of the remaining bacon. Makes 8 (4-inch) waffles.

**Waffles are good with syrup, but try one of these toppings for a change of pace.**
**Orange Butter: ½ cup softened *butter* mixed with 1 tablespoon sifted *powdered sugar* and ½ teaspoon finely shredded *orange peel.***
**Honey Butter: ½ cup softened *butter* mixed with ¼ cup *honey* and ½ teaspoon finely shredded *lemon peel.***

# Banana Pancakes

1 beaten egg
1¼ cups milk
1 ripe medium banana, mashed (⅓ cup)
⅓ cup cooking oil
2 cups Whole Wheat Mix *or* packaged pancake mix

● In a bowl combine the beaten egg, milk, mashed banana, and cooking oil.

Place the Whole Wheat Mix or packaged pancake mix in a bowl. Add egg mixture; beat till smooth.

● Bake batter on a hot, lightly greased griddle using ¼ cup batter for each pancake. If batter thickens while standing, add a little additional milk.

Maple-flavored syrup
Toasted shredded coconut (optional)

● Serve with maple-flavored syrup and toasted shredded coconut, if desired. Makes 10 to 12 (4-inch) pancakes.

**Toasted coconut adds pizzazz to everything from pancakes to salads to desserts. Toast a batch in a baking pan for 6 to 7 minutes in a 350° oven, stirring once. Then store it in the refrigerator for last-minute fix-ups.**

**When making pancakes, lightly grease the griddle and heat over medium heat till drops of water dance across the griddle.**

**Dip ¼ cup batter for each pancake and pour onto griddle, spacing far enough apart so pancakes won't touch as they bake.**

**Pancakes are ready to turn when the tops are bubbly and the edges slightly dry.**

# Choice Wines

Make a good meal great with these suggestions for matching food and wine.

**Appetizers:**
Dry sherry
Cocktail sherry

**Beef, Lamb, Game:**
Cabernet Sauvignon
Pinot Noir
Zinfandel

**Fish:**
Chardonnay
Chenin Blanc
French Colombard

**Ham:**
Chenin Blanc
Gamay Beaujolais
Sparkling Rosé

**Veal, Pork, Poultry:**
Cabernet Sauvignon
Fumé Blanc
White Riesling

**Sandwiches, Salads:**
Rosé
Gamay

**Desserts:**
Catawba
Cream sherry

MENU
CANDLELIGHT DINNER
**Steak with Almonds and Mushrooms**
**Hot parsleyed rice**
**French bread**
**Easy Fruit-Topped Cake**
**Wine: Cabernet Sauvignon**

**MENU COUNTDOWN**

***1 Hour Ahead:***
Prepare the sour cream mixture and fruit for Easy Fruit-Topped Cake; chill. Thaw the pound cake. Assemble the ingredients for Steak with Almonds and Mushrooms.

***25 Minutes Ahead:***
Begin cooking the rice.

**20 Minutes Ahead:**
Prepare Steak with Almonds and Mushrooms.

***10 Minutes Ahead:***
Open wine.
Set out French bread

***At Serving Time:***
Stir some snipped parsley into rice.

***At Dessert Time:***
Slice cake; top with fruit and sour cream mixture.

# Steak with Almonds and Mushrooms

| | |
|---|---|
| ● Place steak on unheated rack of broiler pan. Broil 4 inches from heat 8 minutes; turn and broil 7 to 10 minutes more for rare or to desired doneness. | **1¾ pound beef sirloin, porterhouse, *or* T-bone steak, cut 1½ inches thick** |
| ● Meanwhile, in a small skillet cook the sliced mushrooms, snipped chives, and toasted slivered almonds in the butter till mushrooms and chives are tender. | **1 cup sliced fresh mushrooms**<br>**2 tablespoons snipped chives**<br>**2 tablespoons toasted slivered almonds**<br>**2 tablespoons butter** |
| ● Stir in the dry white wine, salt, and fines herbes; heat through but *do not boil.* Serve over steak. Makes 2 servings. | **⅓ cup dry white wine**<br>**¼ teaspoon salt**<br>**⅛ teaspoon dried fines herbes, crushed** |

# Easy Fruit-Topped Cake

| | |
|---|---|
| ● In a small mixing bowl combine the sour cream, honey, and ground nutmeg. Chill. | **⅓ cup dairy sour cream**<br>**1 tablespoon honey**<br>**Dash ground nutmeg** |
| ● To serve, spoon the sour cream mixture over slices of pound cake. Top with sliced strawberries, raspberries, pineapple, or peach slices. Serves 2. | **1 cup sliced strawberries; raspberries; crushed pineapple, drained; *or* peach slices, drained and chopped**<br>**2 slices frozen loaf pound cake, thawed** |

# Greek Salad

| | |
|---|---|
| **1 tablespoon olive *or* cooking oil**<br>**2 tablespoons cider vinegar**<br>**¼ teaspoon sugar**<br>**¼ teaspoon dry mustard**<br>**¼ teaspoon dried mint, crushed** | ● For salad dressing, in a small screw-top jar combine the olive or cooking oil, cider vinegar, sugar, dry mustard, and crushed dried mint. Cover and shake well to mix. Chill thoroughly. |
| **1½ cups torn spinach**<br>**1 small onion, sliced and separated into rings**<br>**4 cherry tomatoes, halved**<br>**2 tablespoons crumbled feta cheese (1 ounce)** | ● In a salad bowl combine the torn spinach, onion rings, cherry tomatoes, and crumbled feta cheese. |
| **1 tablespoon capers, drained (optional)** | ● Shake dressing well; pour over spinach mixture. Toss lightly to coat. Sprinkle capers atop, if desired. Serves 2. |

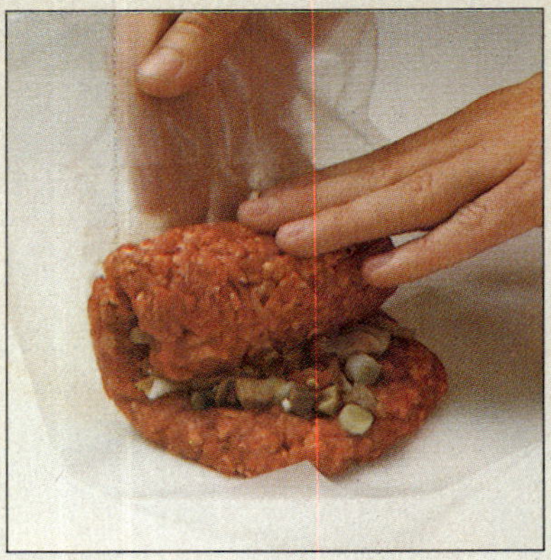

**Roll up ground meat as for a jelly roll, using waxed paper as a guide and tucking in any filling that spills out.**

# Pots de Crème

| | |
|---|---|
| **1 cup whipping cream**<br>**1 4-ounce package German sweet chocolate, chopped** | ● In a small saucepan combine whipping cream and chopped chocolate. Cook and stir over medium-low heat till bubbly. Remove from heat. |
| **4 beaten egg yolks** | ● Gradually stir about *half* of the hot mixture into beaten egg yolks; return all to saucepan. Cook and stir over medium-low heat 2 to 3 minutes more. Remove from heat. |
| **¼ cup coffee liqueur** | ● Stir in coffee liqueur. Pour into two dessert dishes or soufflé cups. Cover and chill at least 2 hours. |
| **Whipped cream**<br>**Grated chocolate** | ● Garnish with whipped cream and grated chocolate, if desired. Serves 2. |

MENU
**International Dinner**
Spanish-Style Fillets
Buttered broccoli spears
Greek Salad
Pots de Crème
Wine: Zinfandel

# Spanish-Style Fillets

**4 slices bacon**

● In a skillet partially cook the bacon. Drain, reserving drippings in skillet.

**¼ cup chopped fresh mushrooms**

● Cook the chopped mushrooms in the reserved drippings till tender; drain.

**½ pound ground lamb *or* ground beef**
**Lemon pepper**
**1 tablespoon grated Parmesan cheese**

● Pat ground meat on waxed paper into a 6x3-inch rectangle. Sprinkle lightly with lemon pepper and salt. Sprinkle the grated Parmesan cheese atop.

**2 tablespoons finely chopped pimiento-stuffed olives**
**1 tablespoon finely chopped onion**

● Combine mushrooms, olives, and onion; sprinkle evenly over meat. Roll up as for a jelly roll, starting from the short side. Cut into two 1½-inch slices.

Wrap the edge of each meat slice with 2 slices of the partially cooked bacon, securing with wooden picks.

● Place meat slices on unheated rack of broiler pan. Broil 4 inches from heat for 8 minutes. Turn over; broil 8 minutes more. (*Or*, grill over *medium* coals 8 minutes. Turn and grill 8 minutes more.) Makes 2 servings.

**MENU COUNTDOWN**

***2 to 24 Hours Ahead*:**
Prepare Pots de Crème; chill.
Assemble Spanish-Style Fillets; cover and chill.
Prepare dressing for Greek Salad; chill.

***1 Hour Ahead*:**
If grilling, start coals.

***20 to 30 Minutes Ahead*:**
Assemble torn greens for Greek Salad.
Cook broccoli spears.
Cook the Spanish-Style Fillets.

***5 Minutes Ahead*:**
Shake the salad dressing; toss with greens.
Butter the broccoli spears.
Open wine.

# Creamy Avocado Salad

| | |
|---|---|
| **1 small avocado, halved, seeded, and peeled**<br>**¼ of a 4-ounce container whipped cream cheese**<br>**1 tablespoon mayonnaise *or* salad dressing**<br>**2 teaspoons lemon juice**<br>**Several dashes garlic powder** | ● Slice half of the avocado; cover and refrigerate. (If desired, dip the avocado slices in lemon juice to keep them from darkening.) In a small mixing bowl mash the remaining avocado. Add the cream cheese, mayonnaise or salad dressing, lemon juice, and garlic powder; beat till well combined. |
| **Milk** | ● Stir in enough milk (about 2 to 4 tablespoons) to make of dressing consistency. Cover and chill. |
| **3 cups torn greens** | ● Serve dressing over greens. Top with reserved avocado slices. Serves 4. |

**With a little ingenuity and hardly any work, you can switch plain ice cream into elegant Peach Melba Sundaes. The recipe is so easy you can wait till dessert time to prepare it. Using 8 peeled fresh *or* canned *peach halves*, place 2 halves in each of 4 dessert dishes. Spoon heaping scoops of *vanilla ice cream* atop the peach halves. Combine one 8-ounce carton *raspberry yogurt* and 1 to 2 tablespoons *brandy*. Spoon ¼ cup of the yogurt-brandy mixture atop each sundae. Makes 4 servings.**

**MENU COUNTDOWN**

***Up to 24 Hours Ahead*:**
Assemble Chicken Rolls Jubilee; chill.
Prepare the avocado dressing; chill.
Chill wine.

***35 Minutes Ahead:***
Bake the chicken rolls.

***15 to 20 Minutes Ahead:***
Heat dinner rolls, if desired.
Assemble Creamy Avocado Salad.
Open wine.

***At Dessert Time*:**
Prepare Peach Melba Sundaes.

MENU
**Jubilee Dinner**
Chicken Rolls Jubilee
Creamy Avocado Salad
Dinner rolls
Peach Melba Sundaes
Wine: Chenin Blanc

# Chicken Rolls Jubilee

**2 whole medium chicken breasts (1½ pounds)**

● Skin, halve lengthwise, and bone chicken breasts (see tips, right and on page 42). Place *each* piece of chicken between two pieces of clear plastic wrap. Working from center to edges, pound with a meat mallet, forming a rectangle ⅛ inch thick. Remove clear plastic wrap. Sprinkle meat with salt and pepper.

**½ of an 8-ounce can (½ cup) whole cranberry sauce**
**⅛ teaspoon ground ginger**

● Combine whole cranberry sauce and ginger. Spoon 2 tablespoons of the cranberry mixture on *each* chicken piece. Fold in sides; roll up as for jelly roll, pressing edges together to enclose filling. Secure with wooden picks.

**1 tablespoon butter *or* margarine, melted**
**⅓ cup finely crushed wheat crackers**
**1 teaspoon dried parsley flakes**
**½ teapoon paprika**

● Brush chicken lightly with the melted butter or margarine. Combine the crushed crackers, dried parsley flakes, and paprika; roll chicken in cracker mixture to coat. Place chicken in a 10x6x2-inch baking dish. Bake, uncovered, in a 350° oven for 30 to 35 minutes. Remove wooden picks. Makes 4 servings.

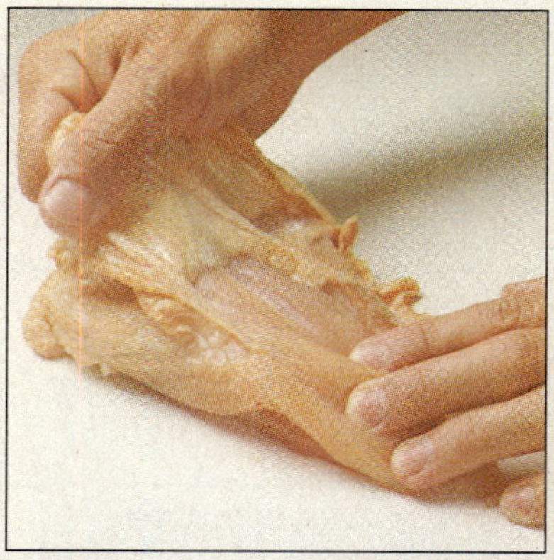

**Firmly grasp the skin of each chicken breast with one hand and anchor the meat with the other. Pull the skin away and discard. Halve breast.**

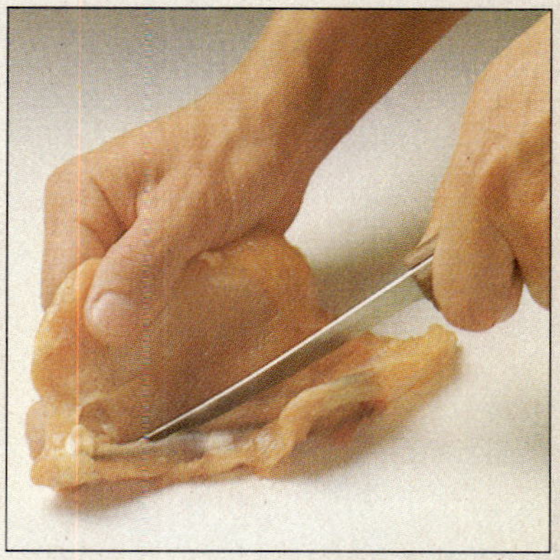

**Hold breast bone-side down. Using a sharp knife, cut the meat away from the bone, working from the breastbone-side out.**

**Place the meat between two pieces of clear plastic wrap. Using the fine-toothed side of a meat mallet, pound lightly, forming a rectangle ⅛ inch thick.**

# Horseradish-Beef Sandwiches

**12 ounces thinly sliced cooked roast beef, ham, *or* turkey**

● Wrap meat in foil; heat in a 350° oven for 20 minutes or till warm. (*Or*, wrap meat in clear plastic wrap. Micro-cook on HIGH 3 to 4 minutes.)

**½ cup mayonnaise**
**1 tablespoon prepared horseradish**
**1 tablespoon prepared mustard**
**Several dashes ground red pepper**

● Meanwhile, stir together mayonnaise, prepared horseradish, prepared mustard, red pepper, and ¼ teaspoon *salt*.

**2 medium green peppers, sliced into rings**
**2 tablespoons butter *or* margarine**

● In a medium skillet cook green pepper rings in butter or margarine till almost tender; drain.

**4 hard rolls, split**
**Leaf lettuce**

● To assemble sandwiches, line bottom halves of rolls with lettuce. Top with meat, green pepper, and horseradish mixture. Add roll tops. Makes 4.

**All it takes for an impromtu dinner party is a quick stop at your local delicatessen or the convenience section of a nearby supermarket. By building the menu on food from the deli, you can be ready for company in less than an hour. These sandwiches can be made with thick rye or pumpernickel bread, too.**

# Fruit Salad Dessert

**1 pint creamy fruit salad (from deli)**
**¼ cup broken walnuts**
**¼ teaspoon almond extract**

● In mixing bowl combine creamy fruit salad, walnuts, and almond extract.

**1 cup coarsely crumbled spice, molasses, chocolate chip, *or* sugar cookies**

● Fold in *half* of the crumbled cookies. Spoon mixture into 4 wineglasses or dessert dishes. Top each serving with some of the remaining cookies.

● Chill 20 minutes or till serving time. Makes 4 servings.

**MENU COUNTDOWN**
***1 Hour Ahead*:**
Assemble Deli Antipasto and Fruit Salad Dessert; chill. Chill wine in freezer.
***25 Minutes Ahead:***
Wrap meat in foil; heat in oven. Assemble horseradish sauce for sandwiches. Cook green pepper in butter or margarine for sandwiches.
***5 Minutes Ahead*:**
Assemble sandwiches. Open wine, if desired.

# Deli Antipasto

**4 ounces Monterey Jack *or* cheddar cheese**
**¼ pound sliced Genoa salami**

● Cut cheese into ¾-inch cubes. Fold each piece of salami in half and wrap around a cube of cheese. Secure with a wooden pick.

**½ pint three-bean salad, (from deli)**
**½ small onion, sliced**

● Drain three-bean salad. Separate onion into rings. Mix with bean salad.

**1 medium carrot, cut into sticks**
**½ cup ripe *and/or* pimiento-stuffed olives, drained**
**1 8-ounce jar mild pepperocini, drained**

● Arrange salami-cheese cubes, bean mixture, carrot sticks, olives, and pepperocini on a platter. Cover with clear plastic wrap. Chill till serving time. Makes 4 servings.

**If your local store doesn't carry Genoa salami, you can substitute just about any spicy sliced sausage. Hard or cotto salami are especially good choices. Pepperocini are mild pickled peppers that can be replaced by a variety of other types, such as pickled chili peppers, pickled whole sweet cherry peppers, or hot pickled banana peppers.**

MENU
**Shop-and-Serve Supper**
Deli Antipasto
Horseradish-Beef Sandwiches
Fruit Salad Dessert
Wine Suggestion: Rosé

# Design-Your-Own Pizza

**Thin Pizza Crusts**

● Prepare and partially bake the Thin Pizza Crusts.

**Zesty Tomato Sauce**

● Spread the Zesty Tomato Sauce over the hot pizza crusts.

**1 pound bulk Italian sausage *or* ground beef, cooked and drained; 2 cups diced Canadian-style bacon *or* fully cooked ham; *or* 6 ounces pepperoni slices**
**Chopped onion, shredded carrot, sliced mushrooms, sliced pitted ripe olives, sliced pimiento-stuffed olives, chopped green pepper, *or* snipped parsley**
**2 to 3 cups shredded mozzarella, cheddar, Swiss, *or* Monterey Jack cheese *or* grated Parmesan cheese**

● Sprinkle your choice of sausage, ground beef, Canadian-style bacon, ham, or pepperoni; and onion, carrot, mushrooms, olives, green pepper, or parsley atop the tomato sauce. Then add your choice of mozzarella, cheddar, Swiss, Monterey Jack, or Parmesan cheese.

Return pizzas to the 425° oven and bake for 10 to 15 minutes longer or till bubbly. Makes 2 (12-inch) or 3 (10-inch) thin-crust pizzas.

**Design pizza around traditional toppings such as ham, sausage, and pepperoni and not-so-traditional toppings such as carrots and parsley. If you use onion, green pepper, or mushrooms, cook them first in a small amount of water for 3 to 5 minutes or till they are crisp-tender and drain.**

# Zesty Tomato Sauce

**1 cup chopped onion**
**1 clove garlic, minced**
**2 tablespoons cooking oil**

● In a large saucepan cook onion and garlic in cooking oil till onion is tender.

**1 16-ounce can tomatoes, cut up**
**1 6-ounce can tomato paste**
**2 tablespoons snipped parsley**
**1 bay leaf**
**2 teaspoons dried basil, crushed**
**1 teaspoon dried oregano, crushed**
**Dash bottled hot pepper sauce**

● Add *undrained* tomatoes, tomato paste, snipped parsley, bay leaf, dried basil, dried oregano, bottled hot pepper sauce, and ½ teaspoon *salt*.

Bring to boiling; reduce heat. Boil gently, uncovered, for 25 to 30 minutes or till tomato sauce reaches desired consistency, stirring occasionally. Remove bay leaf from the sauce. Makes 2¼ cups.

**Herbs and hot pepper sauce give this Zesty Tomato Sauce a flavor that's just right for pizza. Make it ahead and freeze or refrigerate until you're ready to make pizza.**

# Thin Pizza Crusts

Vigorously beat the dough mixture with a wooden spoon for 2 minutes.

**2½ to 3 cups all-purpose flour**
**1 package active dry yeast**
**1 teaspoon salt**
**1 cup warm water (115° to 120°)**
**2 tablespoons cooking oil**

● In a mixer bowl combine *1¼ cups* of the all-purpose flour, yeast, and salt. Stir in warm water and cooking oil.

Beat at low speed with electric mixer for ½ minute, scraping bowl constantly. Beat 3 minutes at high speed.

Stir in as much remaining flour as you can mix in with a spoon.

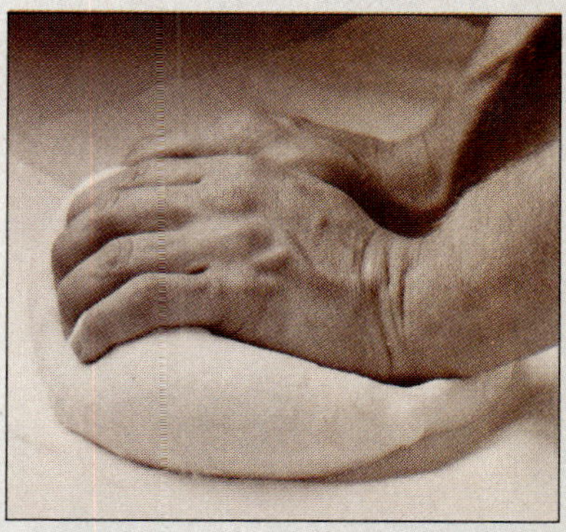

Knead on a floured surface till dough is smooth.

● Turn out onto a lightly floured surface. Knead in enough remaining flour to make a moderately stiff dough that is smooth and elastic (6 to 8 minutes total). Cover dough and let rest 10 minutes.

● For 12-inch pizzas, divide dough in half. On a lightly floured surface roll each half into a 13-inch circle.

For 10-inch pizzas, divide dough into thirds; roll each into an 11-inch circle.

Transfer to greased 12-inch or 10-inch pizza pans or baking sheets. Build up edges slightly. Bake in a 425° oven about 12 minutes or till lightly browned.

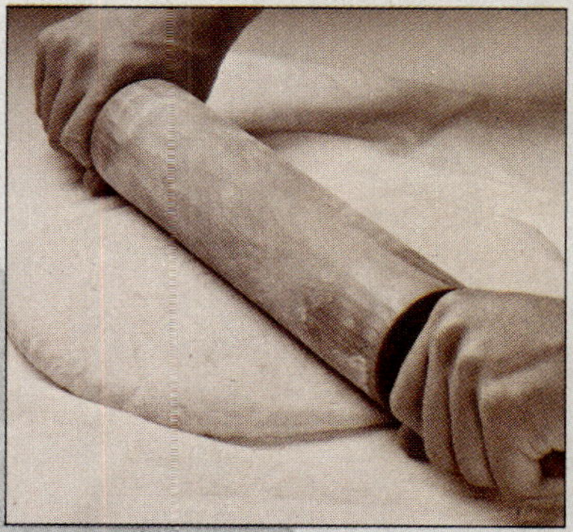

Divide dough into 2 or 3 portions. Roll into circles.

● Add desired toppings. Bake for 10 to 15 minutes or till bubbly. Makes 2 (12-inch) or 3 (10-inch) thin pizza crusts.

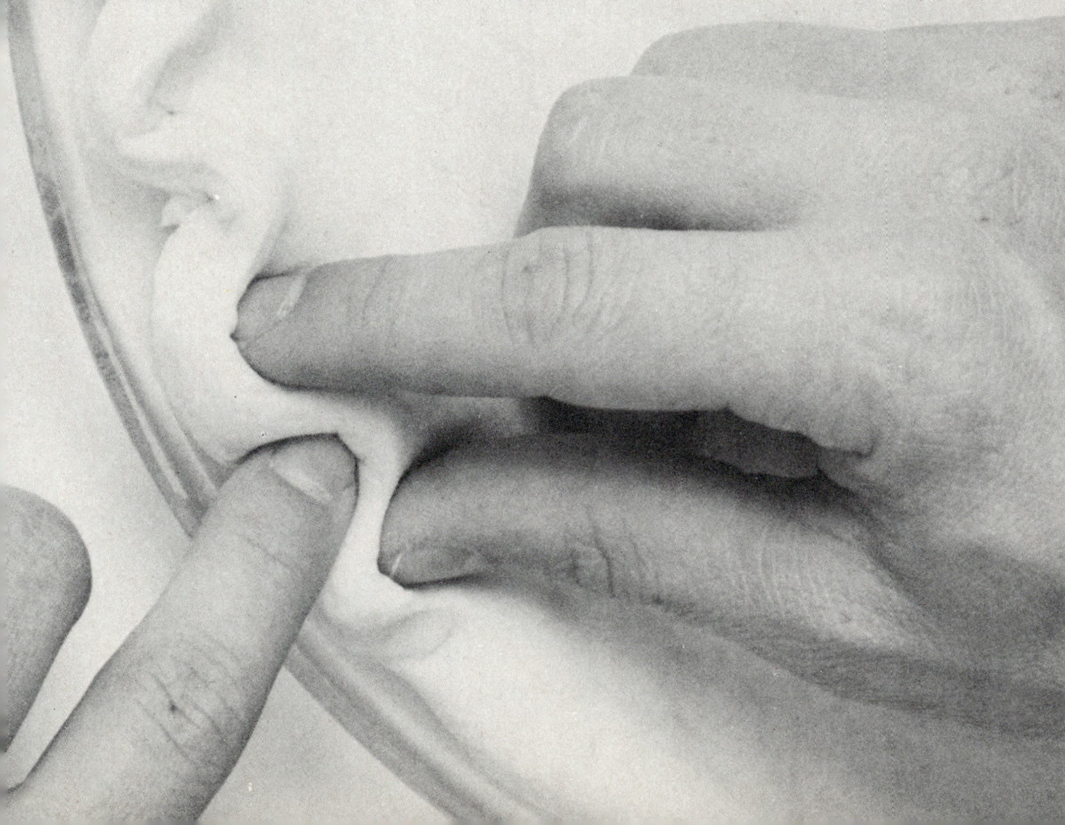

Put circles in pizza pans and crimp the edges by pinching dough between your fingers.

# Freewheeling Sandwiches

3¼ cups all-purpose flour
2 packages active dry yeast
1 tablespoon caraway seed

● In a large mixer bowl combine *2½ cups* of the all-purpose flour with the yeast and caraway seed. Set aside.

2 cups milk
½ cup sugar
¼ cup shortening
2 eggs
4 cups rye flour
Filling ingredients

● In saucepan heat milk, sugar, shortening, and 1 tablespoon *salt* just till warm (115° to 120°) and shortening is almost melted; stir constantly. Add to flour mixture; add eggs. Beat with electric mixer on low speed for ½ minute, scraping sides of bowl constantly. Beat 3 minutes on high speed.

Stir in rye flour. Stir in as much of the remaining all-purpose flour as you can mix in with a spoon. Turn out onto floured surface. Knead in enough of the remaining flour to make a moderately stiff dough that is smooth and elastic (6 to 8 minutes total). Shape into a ball. Place in greased bowl; turn once. Cover; refrigerate 3 to 24 hours.

When ready to use, remove dough from refrigerator; uncover and let stand 20 minutes. Divide dough into 24 pieces; form each into a smooth ball. On floured surface, roll or pat each into a 5-inch circle. Place about ⅓ cup desired filling on half of the circle; fold over other half and seal edges with tines of fork. Place on a greased baking sheet. Bake in a 375° oven for 15 to 18 minutes or till golden. Serve with mustard, if desired. Makes 24.

**Thinking of having a party? These Freewheeling Sandwiches are just right for a hungry gang. Make the sandwich dough before the crowd arrives. Cover and refrigerate it for up to a day.**

**At party time, set out all the sandwich fixings and let everybody mix and match ingredients to build their own creation. (To season each sandwich, start with ⅛ teaspoon dried herb.) The sandwiches are small, so plan on two or three per person. To identify sandwiches, have each guest carve his initials in the crust of his sandwich before it's baked.**

Shape dough into balls. On a lightly floured surface flatten into circles, using your fingers or a rolling pin.

**FILLING INGREDIENTS**
**Choose several items from each category.**

***Meats:***
Use diced cooked lamb or ham, cooked Italian sausage or ground beef, or diced pepperoni.

***Cheeses:***
Use diced American, brick, cheddar, Monterey Jack, mozzarella, muenster, or Swiss cheese.

***Vegetables:***
Use shredded cabbage or carrot; chopped green pepper or mushrooms; sliced olives; or sliced halved zucchini or onion.

***Dried Herbs:***
Use basil, dillweed, mustard, marjoram, oregano, savory, or tarragon.

**Plan on ⅓ cup filling for each sandwich. To make 24 sandwiches, choose 8 cups of ingredients from the list at left. (A pound of cooked meat yields 3 cups when chopped; a pound of ground meat yields 2 to 3 cups.)**

# Jumbled Party Mix

**5 cups bite-size shredded corn, wheat, *or* rice squares**
**3 cups small pretzels**
**1 9-ounce jar dry roasted peanuts**
**1 cup coarsely chopped pecans**

● In a large roasting pan combine the bite-size shredded corn, wheat, or rice squares, small pretzels, dry roasted peanuts, and coarsely chopped pecans; set mixture aside.

**½ cup butter *or* margarine**
**1 tablespoon Worcestershire sauce**
**1 teaspoon seasoned salt**
**Dash bottled hot pepper sauce**

● In a saucepan combine the butter or margarine, Worcestershire sauce, seasoned salt, and hot pepper sauce. Cook and stir till butter or margarine is melted; drizzle over cereal mixture, tossing to coat evenly.

**½ cup light raisins**

● Bake in a 350° oven for 10 minutes, stirring once. Stir in raisins. Cool. Store in an airtight container. Makes 10 cups.

**Jumbled Party Mix is full of tasty treats like nuts, raisins, and pretzels. Make it ahead and serve it as a party food, or take it on a hiking or camping trip.**

# Ham Bundles

**1 package (8) refrigerated crescent rolls**

● Preheat oven to 425°. Unroll crescent roll dough; form into four 6x3½-inch rectangles by pressing perforated edges of two triangles together.

**1½ cups ground fully cooked ham**
**1 medium apple, chopped**
**½ cup dairy sour cream**
**2 green onions, finely chopped**
**1 teaspoon prepared mustard**

● In a saucepan combine the ham, chopped apple, sour cream, chopped green onion, and prepared mustard. Heat through over low heat; *do not boil.*

Spoon ¼ of the ham mixture on half of each dough rectangle. Fold over the other half of the dough; seal edges with the tines of a fork.

**Milk**

● Place on an ungreased baking sheet. Brush bundles lightly with milk. Bake in the 425° oven about 10 minutes or till golden brown. Makes 4 servings.

**Because they're made with refrigerated crescent roll dough, Ham Bundles are truly a short-order specialty. Munch them while you watch television or for late-night snacks. Brushing the bundles with milk gives them a shiny, crisp crust.**

# Nacho Bites

**48 tortilla chips *or* large corn chips**
**½ cup refried beans *or* canned bean dip**

● Spread each tortilla chip with ½ teaspoon of the refried beans or bean dip. Arrange chips in single layer on an ovenproof plate or a baking sheet lined with foil.

**1 6-ounce link cheese food with jalapeño peppers**

● Top each chip with ½ teaspoon cheese food with jalapeño peppers.

● Bake in a 400° oven for 2 minutes or till cheese melts. Serve hot. Makes 48.

**Tame a hunger attack in 5 minutes with this recipe for Nacho Bites. Top each nibble with sliced olive or green onion.**

**MICROWAVE TIMING**
Prepare as above, *except* arrange 12 chips on a plate or glass pizza pan. Micro-cook, uncovered, on HIGH for 20 to 30 seconds or till cheese melts. Repeat with remaining chips.

# Filled Cheese Muffins

**2 tablespoons shredded carrot**
**2 tablespoons finely chopped celery**
**2 tablespoons finely chopped onion**
**1 tablespoon butter *or* margarine**

● Preheat oven to 400°. In a small skillet, cook the shredded carrot, finely chopped celery, and finely chopped onion in the butter or margarine till tender but not brown. Cool.

**1 4½-ounce can deviled ham**

● Stir in deviled ham. Set aside.

**2 cups packaged biscuit mix**
**½ cup shredded sharp cheddar cheese**
**1 tablespoon sugar**
**1 slightly beaten egg**
**⅔ cup milk**

● In a medium bowl combine biscuit mix, cheddar cheese, and sugar. Add egg and milk. Beat by hand for ½ minute. Fill greased muffin pans ⅔ full of batter. Make an indentation in the center of each muffin and fill with a little of the deviled ham mixture.

● Bake in the 400° oven for 16 to 18 minutes or till golden brown. Remove from pans while hot; cool slightly on wire rack. Serve warm. Makes 12.

**With packaged biscuit mix you can make Filled Cheese Muffins in a flash. Stir the muffin mixture just till moistened; it will appear lumpy.**

**For a quick supper, try these muffins with a hearty soup.**

# Hot 'n' Zesty Meatballs

*Pictured on pages 68-69—*

**2 beaten eggs**
**¼ cup beer**
**½ cup fine dry bread crumbs**
**½ cup chopped onion**
**¼ cup slivered almonds, chopped**
**1 tablespoon Worcestershire sauce**

● In a large bowl combine the beaten eggs, ¼ cup beer, the fine dry bread crumbs, chopped onion, chopped slivered almonds, Worcestershire sauce, ¾ teaspoon *salt*, and ¼ teaspoon *pepper*.

**1½ pounds ground beef**

● Add ground beef; mix well. Shape into 60 meatballs. Place meatballs in shallow baking pan. Bake in a 375° oven for 12 to 14 minutes or till done.

**¼ cup beer**
**2 teaspoons cornstarch**
**1 10-ounce bottle barbecue sauce**
**1 10-ounce jar apple jelly**

● In saucepan combine ¼ cup beer and cornstarch; stir in barbecue sauce and apple jelly. Cook and stir till thickened and bubbly. Cook and stir 2 minutes more; pour jelly mixture over meatballs. Keep warm; serve with wooden picks. Makes 60 meatballs.

**Hot 'n' Zesty Meatballs are an ideal two-part recipe. Prepare the sauce and bake the meatballs the night before your party. Store them in separate covered containers in the refrigerator, then heat and serve the next day. An easy way to keep them warm is in a chafing dish or fondue pot.**

# Cheesy Ham-Turkey Rolls

*Pictured on pages 68-69—*

**1 5-ounce jar cheese spread with bacon**
**2 tablespoons finely chopped pitted ripe olives**
**½ teaspoon Worcestershire sauce**
**Dash bottled hot pepper sauce**
**1 to 2 tablespoons mayonnaise *or* salad dressing**

● In a mixing bowl combine the cheese spread with bacon, chopped pitted ripe olives, Worcestershire sauce, and bottled hot pepper sauce with a fork.

Add as much mayonnaise or salad dressing as needed to make a mixture of spreading consistency.

**4 slices boiled ham**
**4 slices turkey breast luncheon meat**

● Spread a thin layer of cheese mixture on a slice of ham and on a slice of turkey. Place the turkey slice atop the ham slice, cheese side up. Roll up jelly-roll style. Slice into ½-inch slices. Repeat with remaining cheese mixture and meats. Cover and chill. Makes 24 rolls.

**Make Cheesy Ham-Turkey Rolls ahead and tuck them away in the refrigerator. For easier serving set out wooden picks.**

# Fluffy Halibut Pâté

*Pictured on pages 68-69—*

**At your next party bring out an assortment of fresh vegetables to serve with Fluffy Halibut Pâté. But don't offer only carrots and celery. Check your supermarket for less conventional items such as fresh asparagus, pea pods, or mild chili peppers.**

**1 8-ounce package Neufchâtel cheese**
**2¼ cups cooked halibut, drained and flaked**
**¼ cup bacon bits**
**¼ cup water *or* milk**
**2 tablespoons toasted wheat germ**
**1 tablespoon snipped parsley**
**1 tablespoon lemon juice**
**1 teaspoon soy sauce**
**1 teaspoon onion salt**
**½ teaspoon dried dillweed**

● Let Neufchâtel cheese stand at room temperature till softened.

In a mixer bowl combine the Neufchâtel cheese, cooked halibut, bacon bits, water or milk, wheat germ, snipped parsley, lemon juice, soy sauce, onion salt, and dried dillweed. Beat till all ingredients are well combined.

Press fish mixture into an oiled fish-shaped mold or a 3-cup bowl or mold. Cover and refrigerate mold several hours or overnight.

**Leaf lettuce**
**Assorted vegetables *or* crackers**

● Unmold onto a lettuce-lined plate. Garnish with additional wheat germ and sliced almonds if desired. Serve with vegetables or crackers. Makes 3 cups.

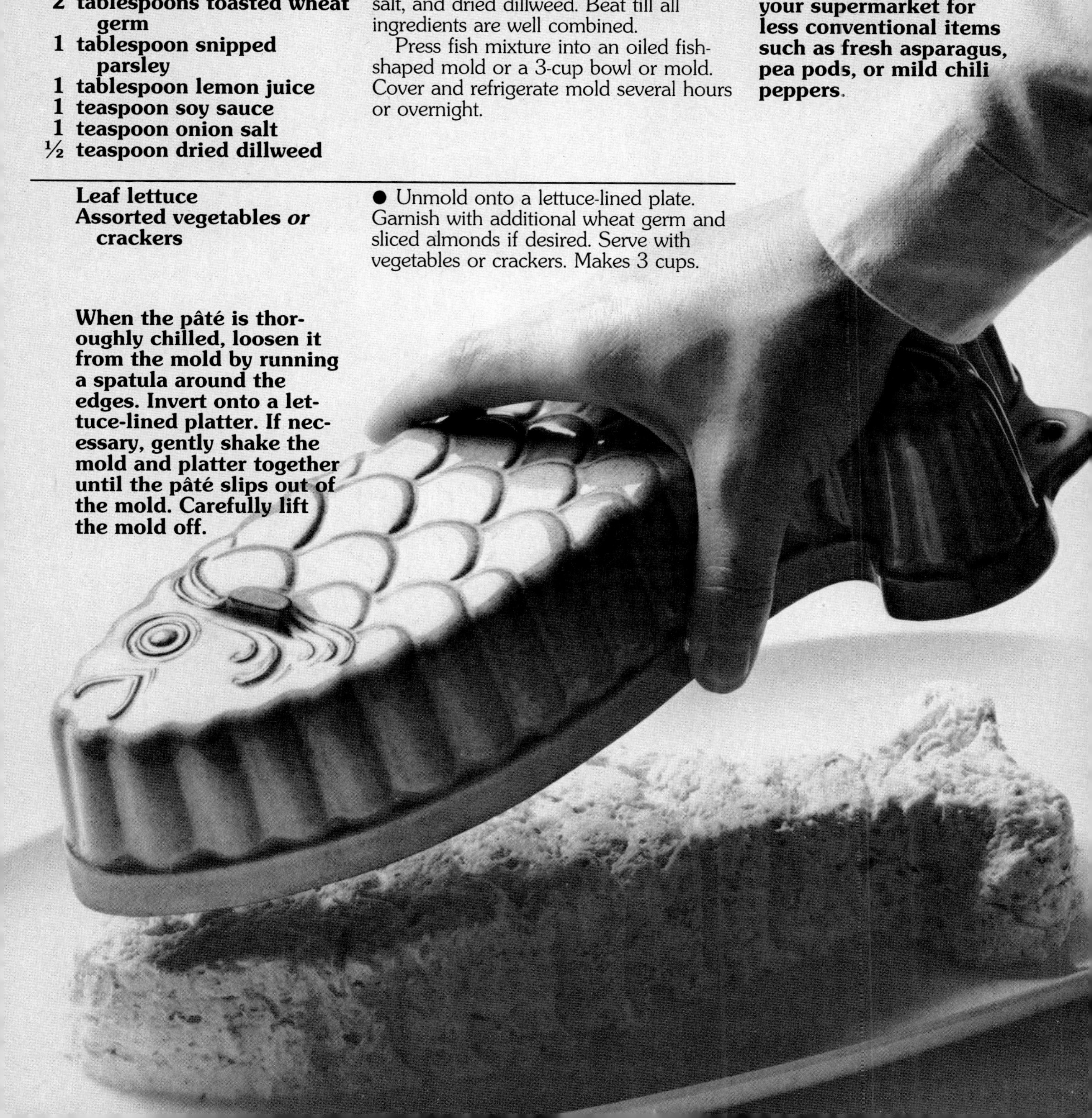

**When the pâté is thoroughly chilled, loosen it from the mold by running a spatula around the edges. Invert onto a lettuce-lined platter. If necessary, gently shake the mold and platter together until the pâté slips out of the mold. Carefully lift the mold off.**

## Potables Aplenty

The party is a winner, but you're running low on booze. Sound familar? Follow these guidelines and you'll never run out again. For mixing cocktails, buy the basics—whiskey, vodka, rum, gin, and vermouth. A 750-ml. bottle makes fifteen $1\frac{1}{2}$-ounce servings. On the average, you can expect most guests to drink one to three cocktails every hour. If you have a wine party in mind, plan one 750-ml. bottle for every 2 guests (one bottle for every 4 guests if the wine will be served only during a meal). For beer, plan one to two 12-ounce cans per hour. Finally, don't forget plenty of mixers and ice.

# Hot Broccoli-Cheese Dip

**1 10-ounce package frozen chopped broccoli**
**1 teaspoon instant chicken bouillon granules**

● Cook broccoli according to package directions. Drain; reserve ¼ cup of the liquid, adding water, if necessary. Stir bouillon granules into reserved liquid.

**¾ cup shredded cheddar cheese (3 ounces)**
**1 teaspoon soy sauce**
**Dash onion powder**
**1 cup dairy sour cream**
**Vegetable dippers *or* crackers**

● In a blender container combine broccoli and the reserved liquid. Cover; blend till smooth, stopping to scrape down sides of container as necessary. Pour mixture into a medium saucepan. Stir in cheese, soy sauce, and onion powder. Cook, stirring constantly, over medium-low heat till cheese is melted. Remove from heat; add sour cream, stirring till combined. Return to heat. Heat through but *do not boil.* Serve in a heat-proof bowl. Or if desired, transfer to a fondue pot; place over a fondue burner on low setting. Serve with vegetables or crackers. Makes 2⅔ cups dip.

**Clockwise from center:**
**Hot 'n' Zesty Meatballs**
**Cheesy Ham-Turkey Rolls**
**Assorted Vegetables**
**Fluffy Halibut Pâté**
**Hot Broccoli-Cheese Dip**

# Choose-a-Flavor Cheesecake

**The brown sugar in this recipe gives the cheesecake a praline-like flavor. To test the doneness of cheesecake, insert a knife near the center of the cake. If it comes out clean, the cake is done.**

**¾ cup all-purpose flour**
**3 tablespoons brown sugar *or* sugar**
**⅓ cup butter**
**1 slightly beaten egg yolk**
**1 teaspoon vanilla**

● Preheat oven to 375°. In a bowl combine flour and the 3 tablespoons sugar; cut in butter till crumbly. Add egg yolk and 1 teaspoon vanilla; mix well. Pat ⅓ of dough on bottom of an 8-inch springform pan (or a 9-inch pie plate).

● Pat remaining dough onto sides of springform pan to a height of 1¼ inches (*or,* pat remaining dough up sides of pie plate); set aside.

**1 8-ounce package cream cheese, softened**
**½ cup packed brown sugar *or* sugar**
**1 teaspoon vanilla**
**2 eggs**
**1½ cups dairy sour cream**

● In a small mixer bowl beat softened cream cheese till fluffy. Add the ½ cup sugar and 1 teaspoon vanilla; beat well. Add eggs; beat at low speed with electric mixer just till combined. (Do not overbeat.) Stir in sour cream.

**Strawberry *or* Raspberry Glaze, Orange Topper, Blueberry Topper, *or* 1 cup dairy sour cream**

● Turn into crust-lined springform pan. Bake in the 375° oven 35 to 40 minutes for springform pan (35 minutes for pie plate) or till center appears set. Cool 15 minutes on wire rack. Loosen sides of cheesecake from springform pan with a spatula. Cool 30 minutes; remove sides of pan. Cool completely. (If you use a pie plate, cool cheesecake completely in pie plate.) Chill thoroughly. Spread desired topper or glaze atop cheesecake. Makes 8 to 10 servings.

● **Orange Topper:** Drain and reserve liquid from one 11-ounce can *mandarin orange sections;* add enough *orange juice* to liquid to make ½ cup liquid; set aside liquid and orange sections. In saucepan combine ¼ cup *sugar* and 2 teaspoons *cornstarch*. Stir in the ½ cup liquid. Cook and stir over medium heat till thickened and bubbly. Cook and stir 2 minutes more. Gradually stir hot mixture into 1 beaten *egg yolk*; return to saucepan. Cook and stir till bubbly. Remove from heat. Stir in 1 tablespoon *butter* and ¼ teaspoon *vanilla.* Cover surface with clear plastic wrap. Cool. Spoon sauce atop cheesecake and arrange orange sections atop sauce.

Cheesecake is traditionally made in a springform pan like this one, but you can also make this recipe in a 9-inch pie plate.

**Blueberry Topper:** Stir 1 to 2 tablespoons brandy or your favorite liqueur into *half* of a 21-ounce can blueberry pie filling.

**We designed this cheesecake to suit your fancy. Take your pick from Orange Topper, plain sour cream dusted with ground cinnamon, Strawberry or Raspberry Glaze, and Blueberry Topper.**

**Strawberry or Raspberry Glaze:** Thaw and drain one 10-ounce package *frozen sliced strawberries* or *red raspberries*; reserve syrup. In a saucepan combine ¼ cup *sugar* and 1 tablespoon *cornstarch*. Add water to syrup to make ⅔ cup liquid; add to saucepan. Cook and stir till mixture is thickened and bubbly; cook and stir 2 minutes more. Remove from heat; stir in drained strawberries or raspberries and 1 tablespoon *lemon juice*. Cover surface with clear plastic wrap. Cool.

# Molasses-Raisin Cookies

**1¼ cups all-purpose flour**
**2 tablespoons wheat germ**
**½ teaspoon baking powder**
**¼ teaspoon baking soda**
**¼ teaspoon salt**

● Preheat oven to 325°. In a bowl stir together the flour, wheat germ, baking powder, baking soda, and salt; set aside.

**½ cup butter *or* margarine, softened**
**½ cup sugar**
**½ cup molasses**
**1 egg**
**1 teaspoon vanilla**

● In a mixer bowl beat the butter or margarine for 30 seconds with electric mixer. Add sugar and molasses; beat till fluffy. Add egg and vanilla; beat well.

**3 cups quick-cooking rolled oats**
**½ cup raisins**

● Add dry ingredients to beaten mixture, beating till well combined. Stir in oats and raisins. Drop dough from a teaspoon 2 inches apart onto an ungreased cookie sheet.

● Bake in the 325° oven for 8 to 10 minutes or till done. Cool 1 minute; remove to a wire rack. Makes 48 cookies.

**Thanks to molasses, these cookies are amber-colored and chewy. If they begin to dry out during storage, place an apple half, skin side down, on top of the cookies in the storage container—it'll help keep the cookies soft. Discard and replace the apple every few days.**

# Peanut Chip Brownies

**½ cup butter *or* margarine**
**2 squares (2 ounces) unsweetened chocolate**
**¾ cup packed brown sugar**

● Preheat oven to 350°. Grease an 8x8x2-inch baking pan. In a saucepan over *low* heat melt butter or margarine and chocolate. Remove from heat; stir in brown sugar.

**2 eggs**
**1 teaspoon vanilla**

● Add eggs and vanilla; beat *lightly* just till blended. (Don't overbeat or brownies will rise too high, then fall.)

**¾ cup all-purpose flour**
**⅓ cup peanut butter-flavored pieces**
**⅓ cup chopped peanuts**

● Stir in flour, then peanut butter-flavored pieces and peanuts. Spread batter in pan. Bake in the 350° oven for 30 minutes. Cool. Cut into bars. Makes 16.

**Peanut Chip Brownies are rich, chocolaty, and so easy to make. Allow yourself about 45 minutes from start to finish. The best way to store these brownies is right in the pan. (Cover the pan tightly with foil.)**

# Nutty Chocolate Chip Cookies

| | |
|---|---|
| **1¼ cups all-purpose flour**<br>**1 cup whole wheat flour**<br>**1 teaspoon baking powder**<br>**¼ teaspoon salt** | ● Preheat oven to 375°. Stir together all-purpose flour, whole wheat flour, baking powder, and salt. Set aside. |
| **½ cup shortening**<br>**½ cup butter *or* margarine** | ● In mixer bowl beat shortening and butter or margarine at medium speed with electric mixer for 30 seconds. |
| **1 cup packed brown sugar**<br>**⅓ cup sugar** | ● Add packed brown sugar and sugar; beat till mixture is fluffy. |
| **2 eggs**<br>**1 teaspoon vanilla** | ● Add eggs and vanilla; beat well. |
| **1 6-ounce package (1 cup) semisweet chocolate pieces**<br>**1 cup unsalted shelled sunflower nuts, chopped walnuts, *or* chopped pecans** | ● Gradually add flour mixture to sugar mixture and beat at low speed with electric mixer till well combined. Stir in chocolate pieces and nuts. Drop dough from a teaspoon 2 inches apart onto an ungreased cookie sheet. Bake in the 375° oven for 10 to 12 minutes or till done. Remove from cookie sheet; cool on wire rack. Makes 60 cookies. |
| | ● *Note:* If desired, spread dough in a lightly greased 15x10x1-inch baking pan. Bake in a 375° oven 25 to 30 minutes or till done. Cool; cut into bars. |

**Here it is, our version of the inevitable chocolate chip cookie. Whole wheat flour and sunflower nuts make these cookies pleasingly different. Bet you can't eat just one! If there are any left over, store them in a container with a tight-fitting lid.**

# Flame It

You'll create an aura of elegance when you present a flambéed dish to dinner guests. To turn your favorite recipes into flaming successes, just follow these guidelines. Place 2 to 4 tablespoons of brandy or other liquor that is at least 70 proof in a small deep saucepan or a ladle. Avoid using a skillet since it is difficult to pour flaming liquids from a large, flat surface. Heat the liquor only to the point of simmering. (Do not boil.) Then quickly ignite the liquor with a long match and pour it over the food. After the flames die down, stir the liquor into the mixture, if possible. Don't dilute the liquor until after it's ignited or it won't flame.

**Of all sweet offerings, a dazzling flambéed dessert, such as Brandy Cream Crepes, is one of the best dinner finales. The crepes and cream filling can be made ahead. But to prevent soggy crepes, don't assemble the finished dessert till near serving time.**

# Brandy Cream Crepes

| | |
|---|---|
| **⅓ cup sugar**<br>**3 tablespoons all-purpose flour**<br>**¼ teaspoon salt** | ● For filling, in a medium saucepan combine the ⅓ cup sugar, the 3 tablespoons flour, and the ¼ teaspoon salt. |
| **1¼ cups light cream** | ● Add cream; cook and stir over medium heat till thickened and bubbly. |
| **1 beaten egg** | ● Gradually stir *half* of the hot mixture into the 1 beaten egg; return all to saucepan. Cook and stir 2 minutes more. |
| **1 tablespoon butter *or* margarine**<br>**1 tablespoon brandy *or* fruit-flavored brandy**<br>**1 teaspoon vanilla** | ● Remove from heat. Stir in butter or margarine, the 1 tablespoon brandy or fruit-flavored brandy, and vanilla. Cover surface with clear plastic wrap. Chill. *(Do not stir.)* |
| **¾ cup milk**<br>**½ cup all-purpose flour**<br>**1 egg**<br>**1 tablespoon sugar**<br>**1½ teaspoons cooking oil**<br>**Dash salt** | ● For crepes, in a mixer bowl combine milk, the ½ cup flour, the 1 egg, the 1 tablespoon sugar, oil, and dash salt; beat with a rotary beater till blended.<br>Heat a lightly greased 6-inch skillet. Remove from heat. Spoon in 2 tablespoons batter; lift and tilt skillet to spread batter (see tip, right). Return to heat; brown on one side. Invert skillet over paper toweling; remove crepe. Repeat with the remaining batter to make 8 or 9 crepes, greasing skillet often. |
| **¼ cup toasted slivered almonds** | ● Fold almonds into the chilled filling mixture. Spoon about 2 tablespoons filling down center of unbrowned side of a crepe. Fold two opposite edges so they overlap atop filling. Place on serving platter seam side down. Repeat with the remaining crepes. |
| **3 tablespoons brandy *or* fruit-flavored brandy** | ● In a small saucepan heat the 3 tablespoons brandy over low heat just till hot. (If desired, pour heated brandy into a ladle.) Ignite and pour flaming brandy over crepes. Makes 8 servings. |

**Quite simply, crepes are paper-thin pancakes, and they're a breeze to make as long as your skillet is well seasoned or oiled and heated to the right temperature.**

**Spoon 2 tablespoons batter into a heated greased skillet. Tilt skillet, quickly rotating to spread batter in a thin even layer.**

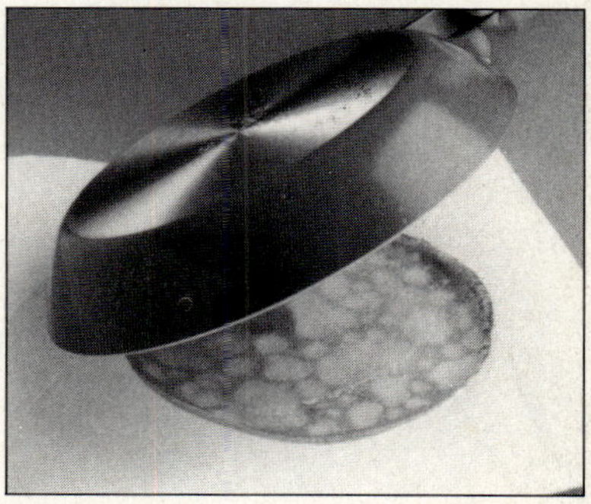

**Cook 45 to 60 seconds or till crepe is lightly browned. Invert skillet over paper toweling, letting crepe drop onto towel. (You may need to loosen the edges of the crepe with a spatula.)**

To serve a warm soufflé, insert two forks back to back and gently pull the soufflé apart into individual servings. Then transfer to plates with a spoon.

# Pineapple Soufflé

| | |
|---|---|
| **1 8¼-ounce can crushed pineapple** | ● Place a buttered foil collar around a 2-quart soufflé dish, extending the collar 2 inches above dish. Secure the foil strip with tape. Preheat oven to 325°. Drain pineapple, reserving syrup. Add enough water to syrup to make 1 cup liquid. |
| **3 tablespoons butter *or* margarine**<br>**⅓ cup all-purpose flour**<br>**⅛ teaspoon salt** | ● In saucepan melt butter; stir in flour and salt. Add pineapple syrup mixture. Cook and stir till thickened and bubbly; remove from heat. Cool 5 minutes. |
| **6 egg yolks** | ● Meanwhile, in a mixer bowl beat the egg yolks at high speed with an electric mixer about 6 minutes or till thick and lemon-colored. Slowly add the cooked mixture to the yolks, stirring constantly. Stir in drained pineapple. |
| **6 egg whites**<br>**¼ cup sugar** | ● Wash beaters well. In large mixer bowl beat egg whites at high speed with mixer till soft peaks form. Gradually add sugar, beating till stiff peaks form. Fold pineapple mixture into egg whites. Spoon into soufflé dish. |
| | ● Bake in the 325° oven 50 to 60 minutes or till knife inserted near center comes out clean. Remove from oven; detach collar. Serve at once. Serves 8. |

**To form a collar, butter one side of a foil strip. Place the strip around the soufflé dish with the buttered side in, extending 2 inches above the dish. Secure with a piece of tape.**

**To top the soufflé with a "hat," trace a 1-inch-deep circle through the mixture about an inch from the edge of the dish.**

**The soufflé is done when a knife inserted near center comes out clean. Move the knife slightly from side to side or the crust may clean the knife as you pull it out.**

# Chocolate-Orange Soufflé

**¾ cup sugar**
**1 envelope unflavored gelatin**

● If using a 1½-quart soufflé dish, place a buttered foil collar around dish, extending collar 2 inches above dish. (A 2-quart soufflé dish may be used without adding a collar.)

In a saucepan combine the ¾ cup sugar and the unflavored gelatin.

**6 beaten egg yolks**
**½ cup milk**
**1 12-ounce package (2 cups) semisweet chocolate pieces**
**⅓ cup orange liqueur**

● Add egg yolks and milk to gelatin mixture. Cook mixture over medium-low heat, stirring constantly, till thickened and gelatin is dissolved. Cook and stir 2 minutes more. Remove from heat.

Add semisweet chocolate pieces. Stir till chocolate is melted. Stir in orange liqueur; cool thoroughly.

**6 egg whites**
**¼ cup sugar**
**2 cups whipping cream**
**Shredded orange peel (optional)**

● In a large mixer bowl beat the egg whites on high speed of electric mixer till soft peaks form (peaks curl over); gradually add the ¼ cup sugar, beating till stiff peaks form (peaks stand straight). Beat whipping cream till soft peaks form.

Gently fold whipped cream into chocolate mixture. Fold in egg whites; spoon mixture into soufflé dish. Chill till firm.

To serve, detach collar. Garnish with shredded orange peel if desired. Makes 10 to 12 servings.

**Chocolate-Orange Soufflé is definitely irresistible. It might remind you of a mousse, since a mousse and chilled soufflé share similar ingredients and their texture is about the same. But no matter what you call it, this is an extra special dessert.**

# Apple Crunch Pie

| | |
|---|---|
| **1 9-inch frozen unbaked deep-dish pastry shell** | ● Preheat oven to 450°; bake pastry shell for 5 minutes; set aside. Reduce oven temperature to 375°. |
| **½ cup sugar**<br>**2 tablespoons all-purpose flour**<br>**½ teaspoon ground cinnamon**<br>**¼ teaspoon ground allspice**<br>**5 cups thinly sliced, peeled cooking apples**<br>**¼ cup raisins**<br>**1 teaspoon finely shredded lemon peel**<br>**2 tablespoons lemon juice** | ● In a large bowl combine the ½ cup sugar, the 2 tablespoons all-purpose flour, ground cinnamon, and ground allspice; add the thinly sliced cooking apples, raisins, finely shredded lemon peel, and the lemon juice, stirring till well combined.<br>Spoon apple mixture into the pre-baked deep-dish pastry shell; set aside. |
| **½ cup quick-cooking rolled oats**<br>**¼ cup all-purpose flour**<br>**2 tablespoons sugar**<br>**3 tablespoons butter *or* margarine** | ● In a small bowl combine oats, the ¼ cup flour, and the 2 tablespoons sugar; cut in butter or margarine till crumbly. Sprinkle crumb mixture atop apple mixture in pastry shell. To prevent over-browning, cover edge of pie with foil. |
| | ● Bake in the 375° oven for 15 minutes. Remove foil; bake 20 minutes more. Cool on wire rack. Makes 8 servings. |

**Apple Crunch Pie lets you skip much of the work of homemade pie because it uses a frozen pastry shell. The apple filling is spiced with cinnamon and all-spice, then topped with oats and brown sugar.**

**To avoid messy spills, place a baking sheet under the pie while it's in the oven.**

# No-Crust Chocolate Pie

| | | |
|---|---|---|
| **2 ounces German sweet chocolate**<br>**½ cup butter *or* margarine**<br>**1 teaspoon vanilla** | ● Preheat oven to 325°. Lightly grease and flour a 9-inch pie plate. In a saucepan melt the chocolate and butter or margarine over low heat; remove from heat. Stir in vanilla; cool. | |
| **3 beaten eggs**<br>**1 cup sugar**<br>**3 tablespoons all-purpose flour** | ● Meanwhile in a small mixer bowl combine eggs, sugar, flour, and ¼ teaspoon *salt.* Beat with electric mixer just till combined. *Do not overbeat.* | **No-Crust Chocolate Pie is a welcome ending for just about any meal. It's deliciously flavored with German sweet chocolate and has a built-in crust that forms while you bake it.** |
| **1 cup chopped walnuts** | ● Fold in the cooled chocolate mixture and the 1 cup walnuts. Pour into the prepared pie plate.<br>Bake in the 325° oven 1 hour or till a knife inserted near center comes out clean. Refrigerate the pie overnight before serving. | |
| **Whipped cream**<br>**Chopped walnuts** | ● Serve pie with whipped cream and additional walnuts. Makes 8 servings. | |

# Malt Shop Pie

| | | |
|---|---|---|
| **1 pint vanilla ice cream**<br>**½ cup crushed malted milk balls**<br>**1 tablespoon milk**<br>**1 9-inch graham cracker pie shell** | ● In a chilled medium bowl stir ice cream to soften; blend in the ½ cup crushed malted milk balls and 1 tablespoon milk. Spread in graham cracker pie shell; freeze. | **If you like ice cream and pie, we've got a treat for you—Malt Shop Pie. For easier cutting, take the pie out of the freezer 10 to 15 minutes before serving to soften.** |
| **3 tablespoons instant chocolate-flavored malted milk powder**<br>**3 tablespoons marshmallow topping**<br>**1 tablespoon milk**<br>**1 cup whipping cream**<br>**Crushed malted milk balls** | ● Meanwhile, in a medium mixing bowl combine the malted milk powder, marshmallow topping, and 1 tablespoon milk. Add whipping cream; whip till soft peaks form. Spread mixture over layer in crust. Freeze several hours or till firm. Sprinkle with additional crushed malted milk balls before serving. Makes 8 servings. | |

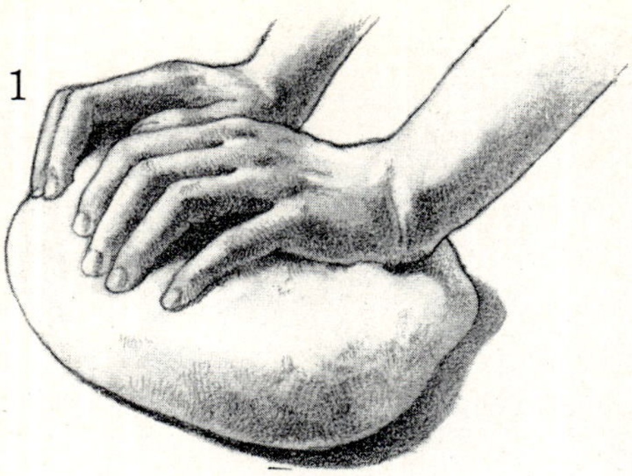


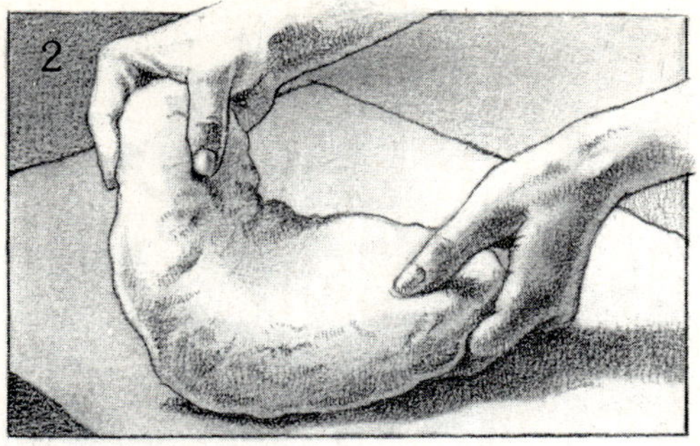


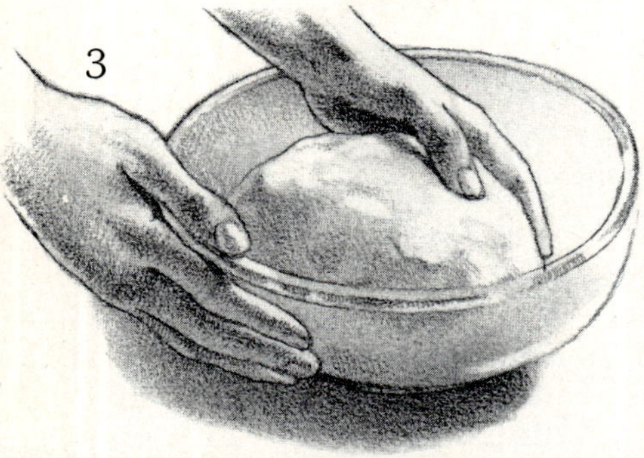

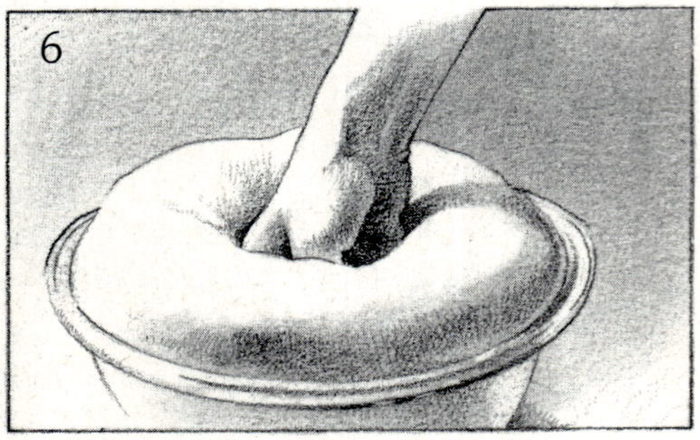


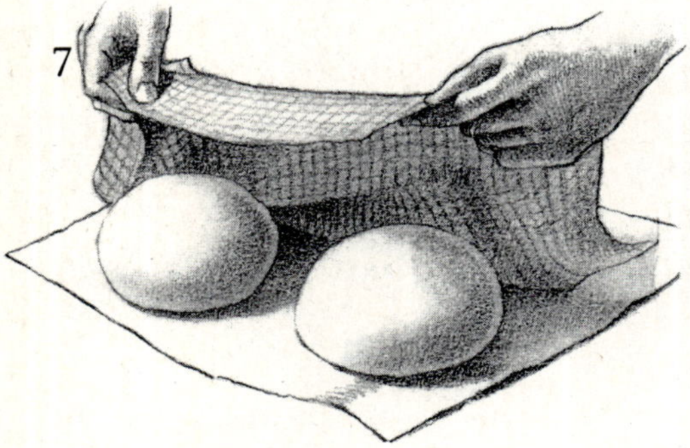


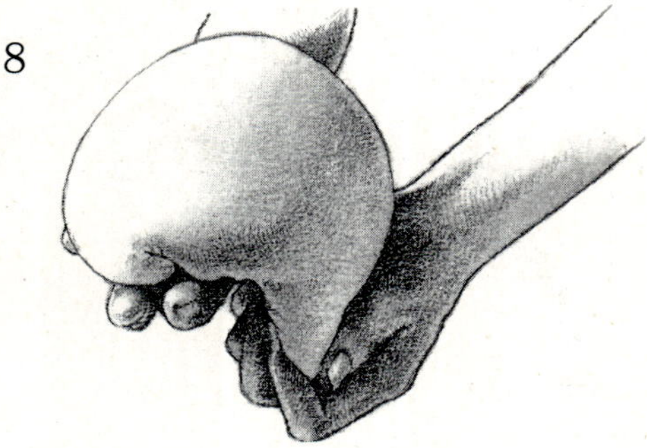


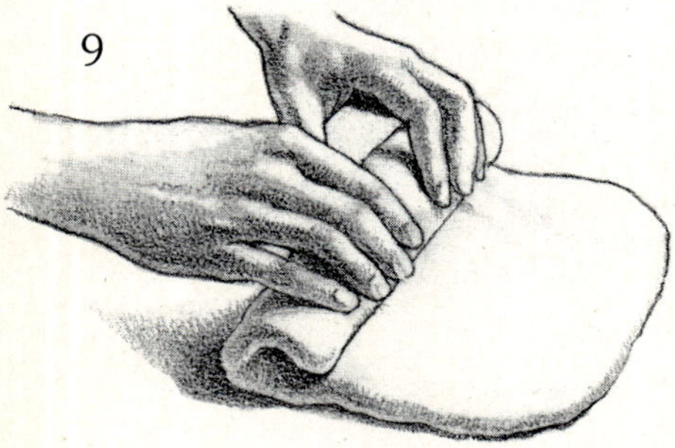


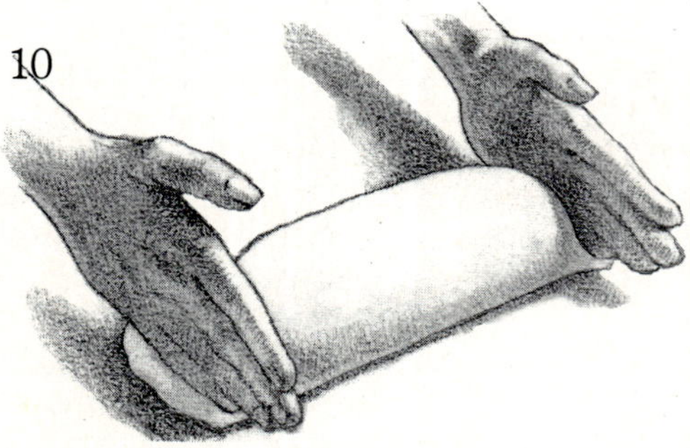


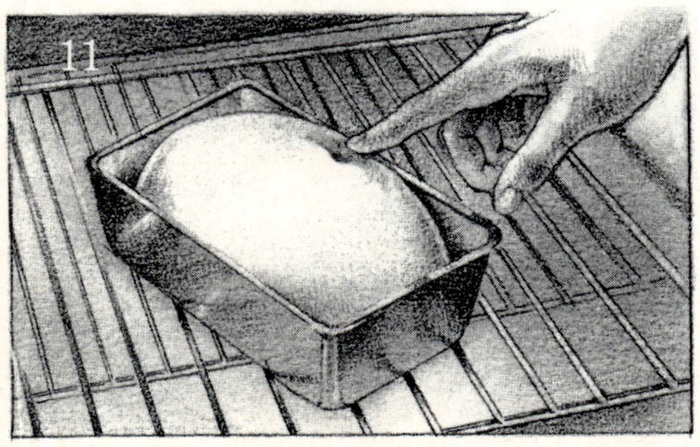


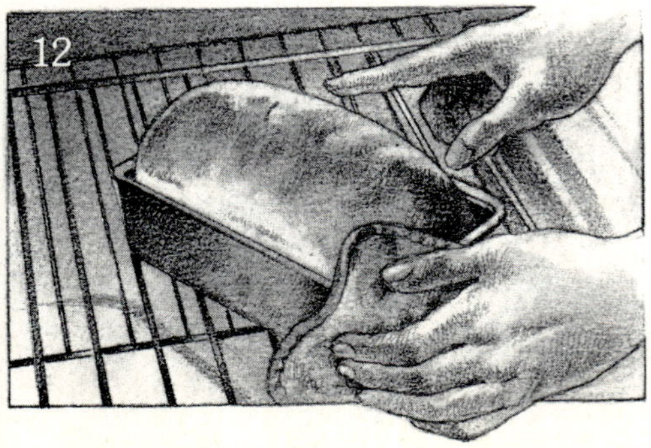


**1** To knead, fold the dough over and push down with the heels of your hands.

**2** Give dough a quarter-turn, fold over, and push down again. Continue kneading till smooth and elastic.

**3** Shape the dough into a ball. Place in a large greased bowl. Turn dough over once.

**4** Cover the bowl with a cloth. Let dough rise in a warm place till double (1 to 1½ hours). The oven is a good draft-free place to set the dough. Place on upper rack with a pan of hot water on the lower rack. Close door.

**5** The dough is ready to shape when you can press two fingers ½ inch into the dough and the indentation remains.

**6** Push your fist into the dough. Pull the edges of the dough to the center. Place on floured surface.

**7** Divide in half. Shape each portion into a ball. Cover; let rest 10 minutes.

**8** Shape each ball into a loaf by patting or rolling. To pat, gently shape the dough into a loaf, tuck ends under.

**9** Or, roll dough to 12x8-inch rectangle. Roll up tightly, starting from the narrow edge.

**10** Seal the ends by pressing down on each end to make a thin sealed strip. Fold the strips under. Place loaf in a greased 8x4x2-inch loaf pan.

**11** Cover the loaves; let rise in warm place till double (about 35 minutes). Touch the loaf with your index finger. It is ready to bake when an indentation remains.

**12** Bake in a 375° oven about 30 minutes. Tap the top. A hollow sound means the loaf is done. If top browns too fast, cover with foil the last 15 minutes of baking.

# Whole Wheat-Cornmeal Bread

**3½ to 4 cups whole wheat flour**
**2 packages active dry yeast**

● In a large mixer bowl combine *1½ cups* of the flour and the yeast.

**1¾ cups milk**
**⅓ cup packed brown sugar**
**3 tablespoons shortening**
**1 teaspoon salt**

● In saucepan heat milk, brown sugar, shortening, and salt just till warm (115° to 120°) and shortening is almost melted; stir constantly. Add to flour mixture.

**½ cup cornmeal**
**½ teaspoon dried dillweed**
**¼ teaspoon ground sage**

● Add the cornmeal, dillweed, and sage. Beat with electric mixer on low speed ½ minute, scraping sides of bowl. Beat 3 minutes on high speed. Stir in as much of the remaining flour as you can mix in with a spoon.

Turn onto lightly floured surface. Knead in enough of the remaining flour to make a moderately stiff dough that is smooth and elastic (6 to 8 minutes total).

See instructions, left, for kneading, raising, shaping, and baking.

# Cheese-Herb Bread

**3½ to 4 cups all-purpose flour**
**1 package active dry yeast**

● In a large mixer bowl combine *1½ cups* of the flour and the yeast.

**1½ cups milk**
**1 tablespoon sugar**
**1 tablespoon shortening**
**1 teaspoon onion salt**

● In a saucepan heat milk, sugar, shortening, and onion salt just till warm (115° to 120°) and shortening is almost melted; stir constantly. Add to flour mixture.

**1 egg**
**2 cups shredded cheddar cheese**
**¼ cup snipped parsley**
**½ teaspoon dried basil, crushed**

● Add egg, cheese, parsley, and basil. Beat with electric mixer on low speed ½ minute, scraping sides of bowl. Beat 3 minutes on high speed. Stir in as much of the remaining flour as you can mix in with a spoon.

Turn onto lightly floured surface. Knead in enough of the remaining flour to make a moderately stiff dough that is smooth and elastic (6 to 8 minutes total).

See instructions at left for kneading, raising, shaping, and baking.

## Bread Problems Solved

If your homemade bread isn't quite up to par, check these common bread-baking problems and solutions.

**Loaves are compact:** The rising time was too short or the liquid used to dissolve the yeast was too hot or too cold. Let the dough rise till your fingers leave an imprint when pressed ½ inch into the dough. Use a thermometer to measure the liquid temperature.

**Loaves are very large:** The dough rose too long. Or, the loaf pan was too small. If dough rises too much, punch down, shape, and let rise again.

**Bread rose nicely, but fell during baking:** The bread rose too long and the heat during baking forced the dough to stretch beyond its capacity. Or, not enough flour was used.

**Bread has a moist layer near the bottom crust:** Too much flour was added during the kneading process.

**Bread has gummy texture:** The bread was underbaked. Or, not enough flour was used.

# Honey Whole Wheat Pretzels

If you're craving a hearty snack or are just out for some fun in the kitchen, pretzel making is something you'll want to sink your teeth into. It takes some time, but you'll be satisfied with the results. These pretzels are a chewy handful of wholesome goodness.

**3 to 3½ cups all-purpose flour**
**1 cup whole wheat flour**
**1 package active dry yeast**

● In a large mixer bowl combine *1 cup* of the all-purpose flour, the whole wheat flour, and the yeast; set aside.

**1 cup milk**
**½ cup plain yogurt**
**¼ cup honey**
**2 tablespoons cooking oil**
**1½ teaspoons salt**

● In a saucepan heat milk, yogurt, honey, oil, and the 1½ teaspoons salt just till warm (115° to 120°); stir constantly. Add to flour mixture. Beat with electric mixer on low speed for ½ minute, scraping sides of bowl. Beat 3 minutes on high speed. Stir in as much of the remaining flour as you can mix in with a spoon.

● Turn out onto a lightly floured surface. Knead in enough of the remaining flour to make a moderately stiff dough that is smooth and elastic (6 to 8 minutes total). Shape into a ball. Place in a lightly greased bowl; turn once to grease surface. Cover; let rise in a warm place till double (about 1½ hours).

● Punch down; turn out onto a lightly floured surface. Cover; let rest 10 minutes. Roll into a 12x8-inch rectangle. Cut into 16 strips, each 12 inches long and ½ inch wide. Roll each strip into a rope 16 inches long.

● To shape pretzels (see photos, far right), start by looping one rope of dough into a circle, overlapping about 4 inches from each end. Take one end in each hand and twist at the point where dough overlaps. Carefully lift ends across to the opposite edge of the circle. Tuck ends under edge to make a pretzel shape; moisten and press ends to seal. Let rise, uncovered, 20 minutes.

After a couple of practice twists you'll see that shaping pretzels is easy. Before baking, brush the pretzels with a mixture of egg white and water so they'll develop a crispy, shiny crust.

**3 tablespoons salt**
**2 quarts boiling water**

● Preheat oven to 350°. Dissolve the 3 tablespoons salt in the boiling water. Lower 3 or 4 pretzels at a time into boiling water; boil for 2 minutes, turning once. Remove with a slotted spoon to paper toweling; let stand a few seconds, then place ½ inch apart on a well-greased baking sheet.

**1 slightly beaten egg white**
**1 tablespoon water**
**Coarse salt, poppy seed, *or* sesame seed**

● Brush with a mixture of egg white and the 1 tablespoon water. Sprinkle lightly with coarse salt, poppy seed, or sesame seed. Bake in a 350° oven for 25 to 30 minutes or till golden. Makes 16.

Shape each 16-inch rope of dough into a pretzel with these step-by-step twists and turns.

# Chocolate-Glazed Pretzels

| | |
|---|---|
| **Honey-Whole Wheat Pretzels** | ● Prepare pretzels, *except* omit brushing pretzels with the egg white-water mixture and sprinkling with salt, poppy seed, or sesame seed. Arrange baked pretzels on a wire rack over waxed paper. |
| **1 square (1 ounce) semisweet chocolate**<br>**1 tablespoon butter** | ● In a small saucepan melt the chocolate and the butter over low heat; remove from heat. |
| **1 cup sifted powdered sugar**<br>**1 teaspoon vanilla** | ● Stir in sifted powdered sugar and vanilla. Add enough *hot* water to make a smooth glaze. Drizzle over pretzels. Add additional water to glaze, if necessary. Makes 16 pretzels. |

Before baking the pretzels, cook them in boiling salted water for 2 minutes so they'll have a chewy texture. Use a slotted spoon to lift pretzels out of the water.

# Two-Way Coffee Cake

- **2 cups all-purpose flour**
- **1 package active dry yeast**
- **½ cup milk**
- **6 tablespoons butter *or* margarine**
- **¼ cup sugar**
- **½ teaspoon salt**
- **2 eggs**
- **Fruit Preserve Filling *or* Raisin Filling**

● In small mixer bowl combine *1 cup* of the flour and yeast. In saucepan heat milk, butter, sugar, and salt just till warm (115° to 120°) and butter is almost melted; stir constantly. Add to flour mixture; add eggs. Beat with electric mixer on low speed for ½ minute, scraping sides of bowl. Beat 3 minutes on high speed. Stir in the remaining flour to make a soft dough. Shape, fill, and bake according to directions below. Makes 1.

**This Two-Way Coffee Cake not only lets you choose between a lattice or cobbler-style top, it also lets you vary the filling. If you like a sweet and fruity coffee cake, opt for the Fruit Preserve Filling. If you enjoy the combination of raisins, peanuts, and cinnamon, try the Raisin Filling.**

● **Lattice Coffee Cake:** Set aside *½ cup* of the dough; spread the remainder in a greased 9x9x2-inch baking pan. Spoon on desired filling, spreading to edges of pan. Stir 3 tablespoons *all-purpose flour* into the reserved ½ cup dough. Roll out on a floured surface into a 9x4½-inch rectangle. Cut into nine 9x½-inch strips; set aside 4 strips. Place the remaining strips diagonally across the coffee cake. Cut the diagonal strips to fit the pan. Place the 4 reserved strips parallel to the edges of the pan. Cover; let rise in a warm place till double (about 1 hour). Bake in a 375° oven about 25 minutes. Serve warm.

● **Cobbler-Style Coffee Cake:** Set aside ⅓ of the dough; spread the remainder in a greased 9x9x2-inch baking pan. Spoon on desired filling, spreading to edges of pan. Dollop small pieces of the reserved dough atop filling. Sprinkle with sugar, if desired. Cover; let rise in warm place till double (about 1 hour). Bake in a 375° oven about 25 minutes. Serve warm.

# Raisin Filling

- **½ cup raisins**
- **½ cup chopped peanuts**
- **¼ cup sugar**
- **½ teaspoon ground cinnamon**

● In a small mixing bowl stir together the raisins, chopped peanuts, sugar, and ground cinnamon.

# Fruit Preserve Filling

- ½ **cup apricot, blueberry, cherry, pineapple, plum, raspberry, *or* strawberry preserves**
- ¼ **cup packed brown sugar**
- ¼ **cup chopped walnuts**
- 3 **tablespoons butter *or* margarine, softened**

● In a small mixing bowl stir together the apricot, blueberry, cherry, pineapple, plum, raspberry, or strawberry preserves; packed brown sugar; chopped walnuts; and softened butter or margarine.

# Vanilla Ice Cream

**1½ cups sugar**
**2 envelopes unflavored gelatin**
**8 cups light cream**

● In a large saucepan combine the sugar, gelatin, and ⅛ teaspoon *salt.* Stir in *half* of the cream. Cook and stir till mixture boils and sugar dissolves.

**2 beaten eggs**
**2 tablespoons vanilla**

● Stir about *1 cup* of the hot mixture into the beaten eggs; return all to saucepan. Cook and stir 2 minutes more. Cool. Add remaining cream and vanilla.

Pour into a 4- or 5-quart ice cream freezer container (see tip, right). Freeze according to manufacturer's directions.

● Remove dasher from freezer. Cover. Pack with more rock salt and ice, using 1 part salt to 4 parts ice. Let ripen 3 hours (see tip, far right). Makes 3 quarts.

# Choco-Mint Ice Cream

**2 eggs**

● In a mixer bowl beat eggs at high speed with an electric mixer about 4 minutes or till light.

**3 cups whipping cream**
**1 cup milk**
**½ cup sugar**
**¼ cup light corn syrup**
**1 teaspoon vanilla**
**⅓ cup green crème de menthe**

● Add whipping cream, milk, sugar, light corn syrup, vanilla, and ¼ teaspoon *salt;* stir till sugar is dissolved. Stir in green crème de menthe.

Pour into a 4-quart ice cream freezer container (see tip, right). Freeze according to manufacturer's directions.

**2 squares (2 ounces) semisweet chocolate, grated**

● Remove dasher from ice cream freezer. Stir in chocolate. Cover. Pack with more rock salt and ice, using 1 part salt to 4 parts ice. Let ripen 3 hours (see tip, far right). Makes 1½ quarts.

**To freeze ice cream (see recipes, left), fill the container two-thirds full. Fit it securely into the freezer; adjust dasher and lid.**

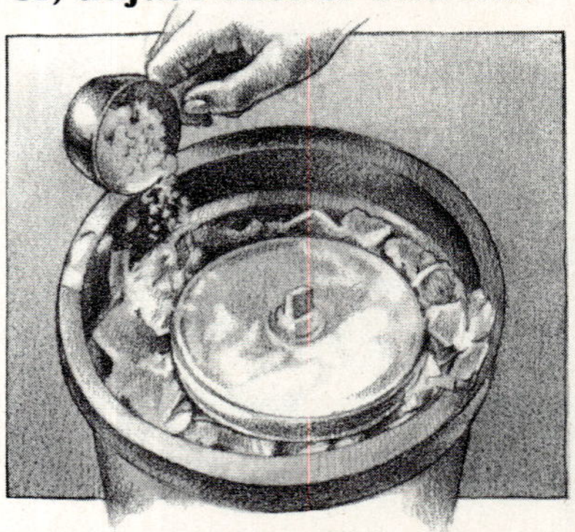

**Alternately pack layers of crushed ice and rock salt into the outer container, using six parts ice to one part rock salt (measured by weight). Fit the handle or motor in place and secure it. Then freeze the ice cream according to manufacturer's directions.**

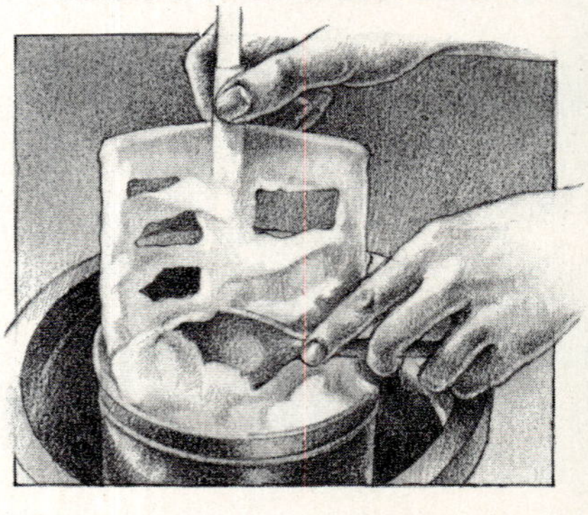

**When the ice cream is frozen, scrape it from dasher back into can. Cover can with foil and replace lid.**

# Chocolate Velvet Ice Cream

**2 cups whipping cream**
**⅔ cup (½ of a 14-ounce can) *sweetened condensed* milk**
**⅔ cup chocolate-flavored syrup**
**½ teaspoon vanilla**

● In a large mixer bowl combine the whipping cream, sweetened condensed milk, chocolate-flavored syrup, and vanilla. Chill well.

**⅓ cup coarsely chopped walnuts**

● Beat at high speed with an electric mixer till soft peaks form. Fold in coarsely chopped walnuts.

● Turn mixture into an 8x8x2-inch pan or refrigerator trays; freeze till firm. Makes 1 quart.

**This recipe features a shortcut to rich, creamy ice cream. Thanks to sweetened condensed milk, an ice cream freezer isn't necessary for Chocolate Velvet Ice Cream. Just whip the ice cream with your electric mixer and store it in your refrigerator freezer until it hardens.**

## Sundae Bar

**Bottled ice cream toppings**
**Chopped peanuts, cashews, walnuts, *or* pecans**
**Raisins**
**Shredded coconut**
**Granola**
**Wheat germ**
**Chocolate, peanut butter, *or* butterscotch chips**
**Tiny marshmallows**
**Applesauce**
**Sliced peaches *or* bananas**
**Crushed pineapple**
**Maraschino cherries**
**Crumbled chocolate *or* vanilla wafers**

Top off your next party with an ice cream sundae bar. Make up two or three batches of homemade ice cream (different flavors, if you like). Set out some bowls, spoons, and a tableful of assorted toppers. Then let your guests concoct their own combinations. You may want to give a prize for the most unusual creation. To get started, choose some of the toppers at left, then add your own.

**To ripen ice cream made in an ice cream freezer (see recipes, far left), pack layers of ice and rock salt into the outer container of your ice cream freezer, using four parts ice to one part salt (measured by weight). Cover the freezer with a heavy cloth. Let ripen 3 to 4 hours. During this time the ice cream will harden slightly and become smoother.**

# Shrimp Egg Rolls and Wontons

- 2 **medium carrots**
- 2 **cups chopped fresh *or* frozen loosepack broccoli**
- ½ **cup chopped fresh mushrooms**
- ½ **cup chopped fresh bean sprouts**
- ½ **cup chopped celery**
- 2 **tablespoons butter *or* margarine**

● Finely shred the carrots. In a large skillet cook the finely shredded carrots, chopped broccoli, chopped mushrooms, chopped bean sprouts, and chopped celery in the butter or margarine about 8 minutes or till vegetables are almost tender. Remove from heat.

- 1 **cup fresh *or* frozen shelled shrimp**
- 1 **tablespoon soy sauce**
- ¼ **teaspoon garlic powder**

● Drop shrimp into boiling salted water. Reduce heat; simmer for 1 to 1½ minutes or till shrimp turn pink. Drain and coarsely chop the shrimp. Stir shrimp, soy sauce, and garlic powder into vegetable mixture.

- 12 **egg roll skins**
- **Cooking oil for deep-fat frying**
- **Sweet and Sour Sauce**

● Fill and fold egg roll skins according to directions for egg rolls or wontons.

Fry in deep hot oil (365°) for 1½ to 2 minutes for egg rolls or 1 to 2 minutes for wontons. Drain on paper toweling.

Serve with Sweet and Sour Sauce. Makes 12 egg rolls or 48 wontons.

**Part of the fun of eating egg rolls and wontons is dunking them in zesty sauces. Plan on serving sauces that offer a contrast in flavors. For example, match Sweet and Sour Sauce (see recipe, right) with Dijon-style mustard.**

● **Egg Rolls** (see photo, near right): Place about ¼ cup of the shrimp mixture just below center of egg roll skin. Fold bottom corner of egg roll skin over shrimp mixture, tucking point under. Fold in the two sides. Starting from long folded side, roll up as for jelly roll. Moisten and seal edges.

● **Wontons** (see photo, far right): Cut each of the 12 egg roll skins into quarters, making a total of 48 (3½-inch) squares. Place a scant 1 tablespoon of shrimp mixture just below center of square. Moisten the top half of square with water. Beginning at bottom edge, roll up as for jelly roll to within ½ inch of top. Moisten edges; seal. Bring the remaining ends together, overlapping slightly; moisten and pinch to seal. Wonton should resemble a "nurse's cap."

# Sweet and Sour Sauce

To make sauce, in a small saucepan stir together ½ cup packed *brown sugar* and 1 tablespoon *cornstarch.* Stir in ⅓ cup *vinegar,* ⅓ cup *chicken broth,* ¼ cup finely chopped *green pepper,* 1 tablespoon finely chopped *pimiento,* 1 tablespoon *soy sauce,* ¼ teaspoon *garlic powder,* and ¼ teaspoon *ground ginger.* Cook and stir the mixture over medium heat till thickened and bubbly. Cook and stir the mixture 1 to 2 minutes more. Serve the Sweet and Sour Sauce warm with egg rolls or wontons. Makes about 1¼ cups sauce.

# Dress Up a Cake

Celebrate with a special cake. And just for fun, conjure up your own idea for decorating it. You don't need special equipment. Frost the cake and smooth the top with a spatula. Then add a few decorations. In the cruisin' design below, start with canned frosting and make the trees from sliced almonds and lime wedges. Then add the message, boat, and water with a tube of decorator icing.

# Chocolate Sheet Cake

● Preheat oven to 350°. Grease and lightly flour a 13x9x2-inch baking pan; set aside.

**2 cups all-purpose flour**
**1 cup packed brown sugar**
**½ cup sugar**
**1 teaspoon baking soda**
**½ teaspoon salt**

● In a large mixer bowl stir together the all-purpose flour, the packed brown sugar, sugar, baking soda, and salt.

**1 cup butter *or* margarine**
**1 cup water**
**⅓ cup unsweetened cocoa powder**

● In a medium saucepan combine butter or margarine, water, and cocoa powder. Bring mixture just to boiling, stirring constantly. Remove from heat and add to flour mixture. Beat with electric mixer on low speed just till combined.

**2 eggs**
**½ cup plain yogurt**
**1½ teaspoons vanilla**

● Add eggs, yogurt, and vanilla; beat 1 minute on low speed. (Batter will be thin.) Turn batter into the prepared pan. Bake in the 350° oven for 30 to 35 minutes or till cake tests done. If desired, cool on wire rack. Then frost and decorate as desired (see tip, left).

**Chocolate Pecan Frosting**

● *Or*, frost with Chocolate Pecan Frosting. Makes 12 to 16 servings.

● ***Chocolate Pecan Frosting:*** In a mixing bowl combine ¼ cup melted butter or margarine, 3 tablespoons unsweetened cocoa powder, and 3 tablespoons plain yogurt. Add 2¼ cups sifted powdered sugar and ½ teaspoon vanilla; beat till smooth. Stir in ¾ cup coarsely chopped pecans. Pour frosting over *warm* cake, spreading evenly. Cool cake on wire rack.

**A greased and floured baking pan makes it easier to remove the cake from the pan. To grease the pan, use folded paper toweling or a pastry brush to generously apply the shortening (about 1 tablespoon) to the bottom and sides of the pan. Add about 1 tablespoon flour to the greased pan. Tilt and tap the pan to evenly distribute the flour. After the greased area is dusted with flour, dump out the excess flour.**

# White Cake Supreme

White Cake Supreme is a light, all-purpose cake that's perfect for decorating. If you want to surprise someone with a cake but don't know their favorite recipe, this is your best bet.

**2 cups all-purpose flour**
**1 tablespoon baking powder**
**1 teaspoon salt**

● Preheat oven to 375°. Grease and flour a 13x9x2-inch baking pan.
In a medium bowl combine the all-purpose flour, baking powder, and salt.

**¾ cup shortening**
**1½ cups sugar**
**1½ teaspoons vanilla**
**1 cup milk**

● In a large mixer bowl beat shortening at medium speed with electric mixer about 30 seconds. Add sugar and vanilla and beat till fluffy. Add dry ingredients and milk alternately to beaten mixture, beating on low speed after each addition.

**5 egg whites**

● Wash beaters thoroughly. In another large bowl beat egg whites till stiff peaks form (peaks stand straight). Gently fold egg whites into beaten mixture. Pour batter into prepared pan.

**1 16½-ounce can frosting (any flavor)**

● Bake in the 375° oven for 30 to 35 minutes or till cake tests done. Cool thoroughly on wire rack. Frost or decorate as desired. (See tip, page 90.) Makes 12 to 16 servings.

# Harvey Wallbanger Cake

Like the drink, Harvey Wallbanger Cake features orange juice and Galliano. This sure-fire combination makes it a cut above ordinary yellow cakes. When you don't want to frost it, bake it in a 10-inch fluted tube pan for 45 minutes, and then add the tangy orange glaze.

**1 package 2-layer-size yellow cake mix**
**4 eggs**
**2 teaspoons finely shredded orange peel**
**⅔ cup orange juice**
**⅓ cup Galliano**
**¼ cup cooking oil**

● Preheat oven to 350°. Grease and flour a 13x9x2-inch baking pan. In mixer bowl combine cake mix, eggs, orange peel, the ⅔ cup orange juice, the ⅓ cup Galliano, and the cooking oil. Beat at low speed with electric mixer for ½ minute. Beat at medium speed for 2 minutes. Pour batter into pan. Bake in the 350° oven 30 minutes or till cake tests done. Cool cake in pan on wire rack.

**1 cup sifted powdered sugar**
**1 tablespoon orange juice**
**1 tablespoon Galliano**

● If desired, frost and decorate. (See tip, page 90.) *Or*, make a glaze by combining the powdered sugar, the 1 tablespoon orange juice, and the 1 tablespoon Galliano in a bowl; mix well. Prick cake with fork; pour mixture evenly over cake. Makes 12 to 16 servings.

# Spicy Pumpkin Cake

| | |
|---|---|
| | ● Preheat oven to 350°. Grease and lightly flour a 13x9x2-inch baking pan; set aside. |
| **1 package 2-layer-size yellow cake mix**<br>**1 8½-ounce can applesauce**<br>**1 cup canned pumpkin**<br>**3 eggs**<br>**¼ cup milk**<br>**1½ teaspoons ground cinnamon**<br>**½ teaspoon ground nutmeg**<br>**¼ teaspoon ground cloves** | ● In large mixer bowl combine yellow cake mix, applesauce, pumpkin, eggs, milk, the 1½ teaspoons ground cinnamon, ground nutmeg, and ground cloves; beat on low speed of electric mixer till well blended. |
| **½ cup finely chopped, peeled apple**<br>**½ cup chopped nuts** | ● Beat on medium speed for 2 minutes, scraping sides of bowl frequently. Fold in chopped apple and chopped nuts. |
| | ● Turn batter into prepared pan. Bake in a 350° oven for 35 to 40 minutes or till wooden pick inserted in center comes out clean. |
| | ● Place cake on wire rack; cool thoroughly. If desired, frost and decorate (see tip on page 91.) |
| **1 cup whipping cream**<br>**2 tablespoons honey**<br>**¼ teaspoon ground cinnamon** | ● *Or* combine whipping cream, honey, and the ¼ teaspoon ground cinnamon; beat till soft peaks form. Cut cake into squares; top with whipped cream mixture. Makes 12 servings. |

**Making delicious cakes is easy when you follow these tips:**
**1) Set chilled ingredients such as eggs, milk, and butter, margarine or shortening out about 1 hour so they'll be room temperature when you start. This way all ingredients will mix thoroughly.**
**2) Preheat the oven to the correct temperature before starting to mix the cake.**
**3) Place the baking pan or pans as near to the center of oven as possible so air circulates freely around them during baking.**
**4) Set the cake or cake layers on a wire rack to cool thoroughly before frosting. This will take about 4 hours.**

# Index

## S



## T-Z



## Tips